MICK & VERONIKA,

WELCOME BACK TO

WASHINGTON!

THE AMBASSADOR

BEST WISHES,

Joe

Also by John Shaw
Profiles of People of World Influence (Algora Publishing, 2002)

Other Titles in the Capital Currents Series:
The $100,000 Teacher: A Teacher's Solution to America's Declining Public School System by Brian Crosby
David, Goliath and the Beach Cleaning Machine: How a Small Polluted Beach Town Fought an Oil Giant—And Won! by Barbara Wolcott
The Other Side of Welfare: A Former Single Welfare Mother Speaks Out by Pamela L. Cave
Torn Between Two Cultures: An Afghan-American Woman Speaks Out by Maryam Qudrat Aseel
Serving Our Children: Charter Schools and the Reform of American Public Education by Kevin Chavous

Save 25% when you order any of these and other fine Capital titles from our Web site: www.capital-books.com.

THE AMBASSADOR

Inside the Life of a Working Diplomat

John Shaw

Foreword by Justice Sandra Day O'Connor

Capital Currents

CAPITAL
BOOKS, INC.
Sterling, Virginia

Capital Books, Inc.
P.O. Box 605
Herndon, Virginia 20172-0605

ISBN 10: 1-933102-16-0 (alk. paper)
ISBN 13: 978-1-933102-16-0

Library of Congress Cataloging-in-Publication Data
Shaw, John, 1957-
    The ambassador : inside the life of a working diplomat / [John T. Shaw].— 1st ed.
        p. cm.
    1. Ambassadors. 2. Diplomats. 3. Eliasson, Jan. 4. Sweden—Foreign relations—United States. 5. United States—Foreign relations—Sweden. I. Title.

    JZ1418.S53 2006
    327.485073092—dc22

                                                           2005031267

Printed in the United States of America on acid-free paper that meets the American National Standards Institute Z39-48 Standard.

First Edition

10 9 8 7 6 5 4 3 2 1

FOR MY PARENTS, JOE AND TERRI SHAW, AND
KATHERINE TALLMADGE

I am interested in the ambassador of a small state. Powerful states need no ambassadors. Their force speaks for themselves. For small states, it matters how they express themselves.

—*Albert Einstein*

The wind and the sun once had an argument as to which was the stronger of the two and they agreed to settle the issue by holding a contest; whoever could make a traveler take off his coat first would be recognized as the most powerful. The wind began and blew with all his might until he stirred up a blast, cold and fierce as an Alaskan storm. The stronger he blew, however, the tighter the traveler wrapped his coat around him and clasped it with his hands.

Then the sun broke out, and with his welcome beams he dispersed the clouds and the cold. The traveler felt the sudden warmth, and as the sun shone brighter and brighter, he sat down, overcome by the heat, and threw his coat on the ground.

Thus the sun was declared the winner and ever since then, persuasion has been held in higher esteem than force. Indeed, sunshine of a kind and gentle manner will sooner open a poor man's heart than all the threats and force of blustering authority.

—*Aesop's Fables*

CONTENTS

FOREWORD

Seen from the outside, the life of an ambassador appears glamorous and exciting. One of Washington, DC's loveliest streets is lined by the majestic homes of the diplomats, each flying their own national flag and hosting events that connect people of influence from around the globe. The ambassadors are seen at many major events in our nation's capital. They appear occasionally on television programs, and are quoted in newspapers. Despite their high profile, however, the daily lives and duties of ambassadors are not generally well understood by the public. Most people can only imagine the events that shape their lives, and that, through their influences, shape ours.

In the pages that follow, John Shaw opens the embassy doors to show the life of a working diplomat. And he shows a genuine picture of that life, rich with details about its scope and nature. Along the way, the reader gets to know one of the most impressive ambassadors to serve in Washington, DC: my good friend Jan Eliasson of Sweden.

I met Ambassador Eliasson soon after his appointment to service in DC. He is blessed with an outgoing personality, a fine intellect, and a compelling smile. He was immediately impressive. My husband and I attended several events at the Swedish embassy, and we invited Ambassador and Mrs. Eliasson to attend several events at the United States Supreme Court. Our friendship grew, and we valued the views of both Jan and Kerstin on important happenings around the world.

My home state is Arizona. As an ambassador for my own state, after a fashion, I secured an invitation for the Eliassons to visit Phoenix. The ambassador spoke at Thunderbird, the Garvin School of International Management. He and his wife also attended a function for some Swedish Americans living in Arizona, and played a bit of tennis with some of my friends. He moved seamlessly between each context, and was as effective on the road as in our capital city.

I suspect that an ambassador of a small country is often more effective than is an ambassador of a large one. Smaller nations are not seen as threats to the power or influence of our own nation, and they can speak out more frankly as a result. Sweden has produced some fine leaders in the past, such as Dag Hammarskjöld and Raoul Wallenberg. Sweden has also shown its leadership more generally by being one of the most generous nations in per capita assistance for development and humanitarian aid. It produces some fine products that are popular in the United States. It also sponsors the Nobel Prizes, which honor the most distinguished scientists and citizens in the world. And this country has benefited from a substantial number of Swedish American immigrants. There are many reasons why a representative of Sweden should be admired rather than feared, and many opportunities for a Swedish diplomat to use his influence to improve the lot of this country and the world.

Now Jan Eliasson has taken on an even more challenging role as President of the United Nations General Assembly. These are difficult times. The war in Iraq, the continuing conflict in Afghanistan, the problems in Sudan, and national disasters such as the tsunami in Asia, the global AIDS crisis, and the possibility of a pandemic flu outbreak pose grave challenges for governments, as for the United Nations. Jan Eliasson has a sensible voice, capable manner, and Swedish talent for leadership that will serve the General Assembly well in these trying times. He will carry with him the talents that he has already displayed, and the admiration of many who came to know him in Washington.

It is a pleasure to read about his life and work, his efforts, and his effectiveness. Through John Shaw's eyes we are permitted a rare look at the many aspects of the life of a successful diplomat. It makes for wonderful reading, and sheds light upon a life that has given much to the world, and that has much more to give.

—*Justice Sandra Day O'Connor (Ret.)*

ACKNOWLEDGMENTS

First, I would like to thank Jan Eliasson for being a generous and forthcoming participant in this project. Ambassador Eliasson allowed me substantial access to his work over a two-year period. He has been engaging, patient, and eager to talk about his profession.

In addition to spending countless hours watching Eliasson at work, I spent more than fifty hours interviewing him about what he was doing and why he was doing it. Most of these sessions took place at the Swedish ambassador's residence in Washington, D.C.

I would also like to thank Kerstin Eliasson for her interest and cooperation in this book. Kerstin left Washington to assume a senior government post in Stockholm shortly after I started this project, so I saw her far less than I did her husband. She was always gracious and open when we met in Washington.

In the course of researching this project, I met with and interviewed nearly everyone in Sweden's embassy in Washington. I would like to thank them for explaining their work to me. All were kind and cooperative. Special thanks to three embassy staffers: Claes Thorson, Monica Lundkvist, and Gunilla Stone. Claes is the embassy's press counselor and has been remarkably helpful in tracking down information and showing me his large archive of photographs of Ambassador Eliasson's tenure in Washington. The photographs in the book were taken by Claes who helped arrange a trip to Stockholm in the summer of 2005, which provided me with valuable insights into Swedish diplomacy.

Monica Lundkvist, the ambassador's personal assistant in both Washington and New York, has always been reliable, responsive, and cheerful in handling my many requests for information and interviews.

Gunilla Stone, the ambassador's social secretary, has also responded to all of my questions with reliable information that was provided promptly and graciously.

I would also like to thank my bosses and colleagues at Market News International where I have worked since 1991. Denny Gulino, the Washington bureau chief, has been encouraging and enthusiastic about the book. No one could ask for a better boss. I would also like to thank Mike Connor, the CEO of Market News, and Tony Mace, our managing editor.

For the past decade, I've been a contributing writer for the *Washington Diplomat*, a fine magazine that chronicles the work of the diplomatic community in Washington. I would like to thank Victor Shiblie, the publisher and founder of the *Diplomat*, and Anna Gawel, the managing editor of the magazine.

I would like to offer special thanks to Kathleen Hughes, the publisher of Capital Books. Kathleen has been an energetic and insightful supporter of this book. She and her team have been a pleasure to work with.

On a personal note, I would like to thank my parents, Joe and Terri Shaw, for their support over the years. Thanks also to my brothers, Dave and Tim; and my sisters, Susan, Pam, and Marybeth, for their good humor and friendship.

Katherine Tallmadge has patiently lived through this project for two years. She has offered a steady stream of insights, support, and encouragement.

CHAPTER 1

Farewell to "Modern-Day Rome"

Ambassador Jan Eliasson in his limo

శ్రా **I** శ్రా

Diplomacy, the ambassador likes to say, is mostly about timing.

So it was with one eye on his guests and another eye on an ominous storm front moving in from the west that Jan Eliasson, Sweden's ambassador to the United States, prepared to say farewell to five hundred friends and colleagues on the back lawn of his elegant residence in northwest Washington, DC.

Combining stamina with charm, Eliasson and his wife, Kerstin, stand for about two hours at the front of a long receiving line, greeting guests as they enter the ambassador's residence. Today, June 6, 2005, is Sweden's National Day, and the Eliassons have decided to combine a reception celebrating this holiday with their impending departure from Washington after nearly five years as Sweden's representatives to the United States.

This party is the unofficial start of Eliasson's last full week as ambassador. It's a week packed with farewell dinners and lunches with professional colleagues and friends, including a lunch at the Supreme Court prepared by Sandra Day O'Connor for the ambassador and his family. A week from today, Eliasson will be formally elected president of the United Nations General Assembly, beginning a new chapter in his life.

The ambassador is dressed in a dark suit with a gold tie and pocket hankie. Tall and lean, friendly and forceful, Eliasson looks and acts like an ambassador from central casting. Impeccably dressed in pinstripes, he has a confident, erect, purposeful athletic stride that recalls Ronald Reagan circa 1980.

Kerstin Eliasson, Sweden's deputy minister of science and education, is in a gray pantsuit. For the past year, Kerstin has lived in Stockholm and worked as a senior government minister. She's returned to Washington this week to help pack up the residence and say good-bye to friends.

The Eliassons exchange hugs, handshakes, and kisses with their guests. The forty-five-second conversation, which the ambassador says is the lifeblood of social diplomacy, is on full display this evening. Jan is extroverted and exuberant; Kerstin is a quieter, more private person. At most embassy parties he works the room like a maestro, while she has fewer conversations, but they are longer and more intimate.

After handling the receiving line like polished professionals, the Eliassons stroll outside to their backyard and mill around for a few minutes under a large white tent, posing for pictures. Several hundred guests are in their stunning backyard, which looks out over several acres of lush green grass, gardens, a tennis court, and an occasional deer.

As the sky darkens and thunder begins to rumble in the distance, Eliasson is urged by friends to say a few words. Uncharacteristically hesitant for a moment, Eliasson decides to speak. He leaves the tent and heads up toward the patio and turns to face the crowd that has gathered in a semicircle. Cameras flash and a single TV camera hovers.

"On popular demand, by two of my friends, I will say a few words," he begins teasingly. "I just want to tell you: thank you very, very much for everything you've meant to us in Washington. Kerstin and I have had the most fascinating, the most rewarding, the most inspiring years that anyone can have. We've been here for two elections, for two wars, one EU presidency, and also for tragedies—9/11 and the loss of Sweden's wonderful foreign minister on another 9/11." He is referring to the murder of Anna Lindh, who was killed on September 11, 2003.

"We love this city, its enormous vibrancy and excitement. You have here, modern-day Rome. Washington, the capital of the superpower of the world. This city has volcanoes under it that sometimes explode. There are so many centers of power—Congress, the think tanks, academic life, the media. And I might add diplomacy. All of us are actors in this wonderful city. This has been a wonderful time for us," he says.

And then he can't resist making a plug for his upcoming job as president of the UN General Assembly. "The UN means very much to me. International cooperation is crucial." Sensing that he has said enough and employing a touch of self-mockery, he declares that it is time to conclude "this short, taciturn Swedish speech."

And then a few minutes later a huge storm, with heavy winds and flashes of lightening, pummels Washington. Some of Eliasson's guests race under the tent while others scurry back into the ambassador's residence. Later, he tells me about his good luck—and the value of timing. "We started our reception at six. If we had started at eight, we would have been in big trouble."

৯ঙ II ৯ঙ

This book describes a fascinating job and an accomplished professional. Ambassadors continue to occupy an intriguing, if ambiguous, place in international affairs, especially in Washington, the political capital of the world. They live comfortable, even privileged lives, often enjoying palatial residences with chefs and limousines and tennis courts. They are invited to elegant dinner parties and receptions, get the best tables at Washington's best restaurants, and are fixtures at the city's high-profile charity galas. They are treated respectfully by politicians and business leaders and deferentially by almost everyone else. Their phone calls are usually returned.

But for the most part, ambassadors no longer negotiate important treaties or pass on confidential information from their president or prime minister to American presidents. In fact, many wonder what ambassadors actually do in a world in which global leaders speak directly with one another, meet frequently, and government bureaucracies increasingly deal with each other without intermediaries. The machinery of global affairs does not turn on the words and actions of ambassadors. Some even question if they are little more than glorified innkeepers for visitors from home.

In truth, ambassadors in Washington play a more complex and varied role than their predecessors did a century ago. They manage embassies, try to get on TV, lobby Congress, explain policies, interact with expatriate communities, give speeches to think tanks, promote companies and products from home, encourage investment, travel to other parts of the United States, and monitor their country's relationship with the most important country in the world.

For nearly a decade, I've been writing about Washington's diplomatic community and have become increasingly intrigued by the role of the ambassador. Most countries send their most experienced, savvy, and polished diplomats to Washington. I've often wondered what distinguishes an average ambassador from a good ambassador and a good ambassador from a great one. How does one measure success in diplomacy?

৯৯ III ৯৯

There are, of course, many possible ways to examine the job of the ambassador. I decided to closely follow the work of one of Washington's best.

Jan Eliasson was Sweden's ambassador to the United States for five dramatic and consequential years, from September 2000 to July 2005. He arrived just a few months before the historically contentious 2000 presidential election and worked here through 9/11, the Iraq and Afghanistan wars, unprecedented strains in the relationship between the United States and Europe, and the 2004 elections.

I met him shortly after he arrived in Washington, spoke to him on several occasions, and noted with interest his reputation as one of the city's most polished and impressive envoys. I approached Eliasson in late 2003 about using him as the framework for a book about the role of the modern ambassador in Washington. We discussed the idea in his office, and I later sent him a detailed memo outlining the broad parameters of the project. He thought about it, checked with colleagues in Stockholm, and then we agreed in January of 2004 to go forward.

I chose Eliasson for several reasons. He was widely regarded as one of the most skilled and accomplished diplomats in Washington. Eliasson's career has been remarkably wide-ranging and impressive. He has held senior positions in the Swedish Foreign Ministry and the United Nations and served as Sweden's ambassador to the United Nations. He also has a deep connection to the United States that began as an exchange student in Indiana in the late 1950s, included a stint as a senior diplomat in Washington in the 1970s, and culminated with his appointment as ambassador in 2000. One of his daughters was born in the United States, another studied here and now lives in Washington.

Eliasson combines classical European diplomacy with the more freewheeling and informal diplomacy that is a feature of Washington. You get the feeling you could transport Eliasson back to the Congress of Vienna in the nineteenth century and he would hold his own—in the formal negotiations, in the side conversations in hallways, in the parlors, and even on the dance floor.

But he can also banter with the best of Washington about the most recent episode of *The Sopranos,* the strengths and weaknesses of Serena Williams's tennis game, the case against preemptive war, and pending legislation in Congress. Witty and charming, Eliasson is also substantive and smart.

When I met with Eliasson about the project, he was entering the final years of his forty-year diplomatic career. He had a wealth of experience, a broad perspective, and the willingness to look back and reflect. And he could afford to be more candid than most diplomats. He was not worried about his next promotion. "I guess they won't be able to fire me if I tell you what I think," he teased on several occasions. But I never had the feeling that he told me more than he wanted to.

Eliasson agrees that the job of ambassador is a mystery to many and there is considerable value in lifting the veil. He has long believed the public should better understand how diplomacy really works.

My approach in writing about the ambassador has been simple—to watch, listen, and ask questions. Eliasson provided me with remarkable access to him and his embassy for the final year and a half of his tenure in Washington, starting in January 2004 until he left in July 2005.

As a result, I've seen him in dozens of contexts: escorting two Swedish foreign ministers around Washington, testifying before Congress, and captivating a group of Capitol Hill interns about the life and legacy of one of Sweden's humanitarian giants, Raoul Wallenberg.

I've observed Eliasson at receptions at his residence, at two briefings for the American winners of Nobel Prizes, at several think tank seminars, and at a waterfront festival commemorating a former Swedish colony that was built in the Delaware valley.

I've watched him inspire a class of graduate students about the art of negotiation and diplomacy, arrange an elegant dinner for his fellow Swede Hans Blix, preside over the embassy's morning staff meeting, host a dinner before the Opera Ball, and preside over a reception in which he awarded Sweden's Polar Star to a former American diplomat.

I've seen him lecture on UN reform, speak with interns, organize a Santa Lucia Christmastime procession, chat up the chief justice, play with his young grandson, and tear up as a group of young Swedish singers sang a nostalgic song about the end of a school year and the start of summer.

I've listened as he has vividly described encounters with Saddam Hussein, Pope John Paul II, Serena and Venus Williams, Kofi Annan, Bill Clinton, George W. Bush, Paul Wolfowitz, Madeleine Albright, Colin Powell, and Condoleezza Rice.

I talked with him privately for nearly fifty hours and read almost everything he has written in English. I interviewed nearly one hundred people about Eliasson, including other diplomats in Washington, staff at the embassy, and leaders in Washington's diplomatic community.

In the summer of 2005, I traveled to Stockholm to interview other Swedish diplomats, senior members of Sweden's parliament, and various experts in diplomacy to get a better sense of Eliasson's work and reputation back home.

As this book will show, during his five years in Washington, Eliasson ascended to the top tier of Washington diplomacy, employing heavy doses of charm and substance. Sweden's ambassador in Washington does not automatically get placed on Washington's A-list. It takes work and planning and some luck. In ways subtle and overt, Eliasson came to embody Swedish diplomacy for the people in Washington. He offered a vision of the world that many found compelling, others saw as poetic, and some dismissed as quaint. He tried to walk some very delicate lines: being idealistic without being pedantic or hectoring, hopeful without seeming naive, visionary without seeming impractical, fun and stylish—yet also serious and substantive.

He did all of this in a distinctly un-Swedish way: he was outgoing, gregarious, aggressive, passionate, talkative, and sentimental. The Jan Eliasson I've seen is intensely driven and very ambitious—but his ambition is carried lightly in public and is tightly focused on professional excellence. For him, diplomacy is a high calling, an honorable profession, and enormous fun.

"Being a diplomat," he said, "is my first identity."

He can take over a room or fade into the background, depending on what the situation requires. He enjoys being at the center of things, but he has a keen sense of what each situation requires. With equal skill, he can play Clark Kent or Superman. He is charming and exuberant and laughs easily. He is an excellent mimic who can do a wonderful Henry Kissinger imitation. But when tired or frustrated or angry, he can be cool, cryptic, and cranky.

At sixty-five and near the end of his formal career, he is more idealistic and optimistic than many people are in their twenties. But it's an idealism and optimism tempered by hard experiences in war zones, hell holes, and refugee camps.

Eliasson, I came to appreciate, would be great to have at your side in a conflict; but not in the sense that he would be a fierce, brass-knuckled, anything-goes advocate. He would be a tough, resourceful, creative, and principled supporter. He is someone you would trust to mediate a dispute, confident that he would be fair and just to all parties.

The ambassador would be the perfect seat mate on a long transatlantic flight—interesting, engaging, fun, but also respectful of your personal space and quick to anticipate when you wanted to dip into your book or watch the movie.

His dream job, he once told me, would be a United States senator. I took that to mean that he was attracted to the job in its classic sense: to be a fair-minded, far-seeing statesman who addressed his country's challenges with wisdom and probity. A career diplomat, Eliasson has the temperament and skills of a professional politician. I've seen him work a festival of Swedish Americans in a way that Bill Clinton would have admired.

"Jan Eliasson," one Swedish journalist told me, "is the best politician in Sweden who has never run for office."

The ambassador, I've found, often reveals himself most when speaking about others. In Washington, he spoke frequently of Anna Lindh, Raoul Wallenberg, and Dag Hammarskjöld. Hammarskjöld, in Eliasson's view, is the embodiment of a superb Swedish civil servant who, when given a larger platform, became a global statesman and a legendary secretary general of the United Nations. In Wallenberg, he saw the conscience of Sweden: a young man willing to set aside a life of wealth and privilege and risk everything for a noble cause. And in Lindh, he saw a charismatic stateswoman—full of energy and idealism and toughness, the Swedish ideal come alive and then cut short in the twenty-first century.

Eliasson is a sincere man and an operator. He seems to like all people, but especially interesting, accomplished, ambitious, and attractive people.

A self-described technophobe, he organizes his life around scrawled notes on scraps of paper and a small, black pocket calendar. But with the help of his indefatigable personal assistant, Monica Lundkvist, he seems to keep track of everything, remember everyone, and follow up on all his commitments.

He is curious and inquisitive and open to new ideas. His interests range from high to low culture. He loves classical music, also Westerns and tennis.

He knows how to connect with people and can banter with the best. He chatted with Colin Powell about Volvos and ABBA and with Condoleezza Rice about playing the piano, his wife's passion.

The ambassador is an aggressive, even relentless, networker. But he has near-perfect tone and pitch. I've never seen him ingratiate or pander. I recall watching him chat with Chief Justice William Rehnquist, a proud Swedish American, at the embassy's Santa Lucia Christmas party. He was friendly and solicitous, but in no way fawning or obsequious.

He is a competitive and a proud person. On many occasions I heard him describe an event or dinner by saying, "I was the only ambassador there."

The ambassador is respected and liked in Sweden. He is seen as accomplished, accessible, and both willing and able to explain the complexities of international affairs so average citizens can understand. Some in Stockholm criticize him for being too public, a self-promoter, and self-absorbed. "He's become so American," one senior Swedish parliamentarian told me, not appearing to intend the comment as a compliment.

During his time in Washington, Eliasson was a skilled, successful, and constructive ambassador. Better than most of his colleagues, he understood how power flows in Washington, who makes decisions, and how to influence them.

Given Sweden's modest role in the world, he never dominated Washington's diplomatic scene like Prince Bandar bin Sultan of Saudi Arabia, who represented his nation from 1982 to 2005, or Anatolyn Dobrynin, the former Soviet ambassador, who served in Washington from 1962 to 1986.

As this book will show, Eliasson made quiet but significant contributions during his time in Washington. He was a colorful, interesting, and positive force. But I will not give him a weight or significance that is not borne out by the facts. The ambassador gave Sweden prominence and visibility in Washington and presented views that were more interesting, nuanced, active, and tough-minded than many expected.

He offered a Swedish view of the world that emphasized the sanctity of international law, the importance of the United Nations, and the wisdom of multilateralism. This vision was shared rhetorically by the Clinton administration, but almost not at all by the Bush administration. But Eliasson kept at it, constantly looking for ways to bring the worldviews of America and Europe into closer alignment.

He reached out creatively and energetically to Swedish Americans, a large, successful extended community of nearly ten million. He skillfully tapped into their American and Swedish identities, and emphasized that both were fully compatible. At a farewell lunch for Eliasson at the Swedish American Chamber of Commerce, the audience was largely Swedish American. They beamed as he spoke, palpably proud of the elegant, smooth, and successful man who represented their homeland.

Eliasson tried to offer what he called a reasonable European perspective about the world, and aspired to serve as a bridge between Europe and the United States during a tense and difficult time. He shared many European criticisms of the United States, but believed the world works best when America and Europe are close partners.

Eliasson focused intensely on the bilateral relationship between Sweden and the United States. He was determined to anticipate possible tensions, prevent misunderstandings, communicate clearly, and confront problems that arose.

Like virtually all other modern ambassadors, Eliasson did not shape war and peace. He did not negotiate treaties that will endure for decades or craft doctrines that will last for a generation. But he understood the many roles a modern ambassador must play and performed them well. On one day he could speak with eloquence and passion in the East Room of the White House about the Nobel Prize and the next day carry the pink purse of Swedish defense minister Leni Björklund, into the Pentagon, several steps behind Donald Rumsfeld and her. He worked diligently and creatively to represent his country and to shape some of the policy debates that unfolded in Washington.

Through it all, Eliasson gave diplomacy a good name, showing young diplomats that their profession could be consequential and fun and a high calling. He did everything he could to make sure Sweden was visible, noticed, and respected in Washington—and was given a seat at the table.

CHAPTER 2

Ambassadors in the Modern World

Several members of the Eliasson family with President Clinton as Jan presents his credentials

ॐ **I** ॐ

Ottaviano Maggi, writing in 1596, set a high standard for what it takes to be an ambassador.

"An ambassador should be a trained theologian, should be well-versed in Aristotle and Plato, and should be able at a moment's notice to solve the most abstruse problems in correct dialectical form; he should also be expert in mathematics, architecture, music, physics, and civil and canon law," he declared. "He should speak and write Latin fluently and must also be proficient in Greek, Spanish, French, German and Turkish. While being a trained classical scholar, a historian, a geographer, and an expert in military science, he must also have a cultured taste for poetry. And above all he must be of excellent family, rich and endowed with a fine physical presence." (Mayer, *The Diplomats*)

Serving as personal emissaries from one leader to another, ambassadors were once crucial players in international relations. They negotiated serious and often secret agreements. They conducted high-stakes negotiations that sometimes prevented, and sometimes provoked, wars.

The seventeenth-century jurist Grotius referred reverentially to the "sacredness of ambassadors." But others have observed that the word "ambassador" comes from the Latin word "ambactus," which means "vassal" or "dependent"—a noticeably less exalted designation.

An ambassador, according to the *Diplomat's Dictionary,* is a diplomatic agent of the highest rank, accredited to a foreign sovereign or international organization as the resident representative of his own government. For millennia, leaders of one empire or nation have sent representatives to convey and receive information from leaders of other political entities. Whether called agents, orators, negotiators, messengers, or ambassadors, they were important instruments in the conduct of business between states.

Historians say envoys have been at work since the dawn of history. In classical Greece, ambassadors did not live in the cities they were sent to, and their status was decidedly middling. One historian has noted that in classical Athens, ambassadors, while on a mission abroad, were paid about the same as stonemasons.

"But it was probably not finance that dissuaded men so much as the danger that they would be repudiated or punished for their work—and the lack of comfort and protection in their travels. This was to be a constant lament of ambassadors down to our times," writes William R. Polk, a scholar of international relations.

Beginning in the thirteenth century, the leaders of Venice began to require their envoys to submit written reports on what they had learned at the end of their missions. The requirement transformed diplomacy because it forced envoys to take a more systematic approach to their missions. These reports converted what had been merely episodic ventures into an organized, or at least, documented process.

Historians agree that diplomacy in its modern form began in Italy in the fifteenth century with the creation of the resident embassy with an ambassador as its head. Ambassadors were sent to another nation, remained there, observed and described events, and passed on messages sent by their home governments. Ambassadors had heft because they were held to have "full representational character" and were believed to represent their sovereigns "even in their dignity." Ambassadors were seen as consequential, even powerful, figures who served as the personal representatives of the head of their state.

François de Callières, a French diplomat, described the work of ambassadors in exalted terms in a classic essay written in 1716 titled "On the Manner of Negotiation with Princes." An ambassador, he wrote,

> indeed resembles in a certain sense the actor placed before the eyes of the public in order that he may play a great part, for his profession raises him above the ordinary condition of mankind and makes him into some sort the equal of the masters of the earth by that right of representation which attaches to his service, and by the special relations which his offices give him the mighty ones of the earth.

De Callières sees diplomacy and the work of an ambassador as a high calling and declares a good ambassador is worth his weight in gold.

> By his industry and application he may himself produce changes of opinion favorable to the office which he has to discharge; indeed, if he do but once in an apt moment catch the tide at the flood he may confer a benefit on his prince a hundredfold greater than any expense in treasure or personal effort which he may have put forth.

The French diplomat also provides a list of required qualities for the ambassador that mirror those of Ottaviano Maggi.

> An ambassador should possess an observant mind, a spirit of application which refuses to be distracted by pleasures or frivolous amusements, a sound judgment which takes the measures of things as they are and which goes straight to its goals by the shortest and most natural paths without wandering into useless refinements and subtleties which as a rule only succeed in repelling those with whom one is dealing. The negotiator must further possess the penetration which enables him to discover the thoughts of men and to know by the least movement of their countenances what passions are stirring within, for such movements are often betrayed by even the most practiced negotiator.

He must also have a mind so fertile in expedients as easily to smooth away the difficulties which he meets in the course of his duty; he must have presence of mind to find a quick and pregnant reply even to unforeseen surprises, and by such judicious replies must be able to recover himself when his foot has slipped. An equable humour, a tranquil and patient nature, always ready to listen with attention to those whom he meets; an address always open, genial, civil, agreeable, with easy and ingratiating manners which assist largely in making a favorable impression upon those around him—these things are the indispensable adjuncts to the negotiator's profession. . . . Above all the good negotiator must have sufficient control over himself to resist the longing to speak before he has really thought what he shall say. (François de Callières)

❧ II ❧

If in the eighteenth century, ambassadors sometimes held the fate of nations in their hands and were viewed as the personal representatives of their princes, the nineteenth century marked the beginning of the process by which the diplomat's freedom was restricted and his functions transformed. With the advent of the telegraph and then the telephone, the era of great ambassadors who were policy makers in their own right ended.

But even if the power and authority of the ambassador were fading, these diplomats still dealt with lofty issues. British diplomat and historian Sir Harold Nicolson in his classic text *Diplomacy*, written in 1939, argues that in the nineteenth century, diplomats still dealt with high politics and would have felt sullied to work on less exalted matters such as commerce. He adds that diplomats were not expected to engage with the public, asserting "it would have been regarded as an act of unthinkable vulgarity to appeal to the common people on any issue of international policy."

The ambassador was expected to entertain in a style commensurate with the dignity of the country he represented. Nicolson placed a pronounced emphasis on the social functions of diplomats, saying a special style was important.

He is expected to entertain frequently, to give large official dinner parties and balls and to invite officials, colleagues and men of business to constant informal meals. He is required to cultivate the intimacy of persons of eminence or influence in the country in which he resides; to display a lively interest in local industries, art, sport, letters; to visit the provinces and acquaint himself with industrial and agricultural conditions; and to keep in friendly contact with those of his countrymen who share his exile.

Nicolson held an exalted view of ambassadors, writing that the essential traits of a good diplomat were truthfulness, calm, good temper, patience, modesty, and loyalty.

"But, the reader may object, you have forgotten intelligence, knowledge, discernment, prudence, hospitality, charm, industry, courage and even tact. I have not forgotten them. I have taken them for granted," he said.

In 1961, the Vienna Convention on Diplomatic Relations codified customary law on diplomacy—clarifying, tightening, refining, and relaunching it in the form of a multilateral treaty. The convention outlined the main functions of a diplomatic mission that was headed by the ambassador. They are to represent the sending state in the receiving state, protecting in the receiving state the interests of the sending state and its nationals within limits of international law, negotiating with the government of the receiving state, ascertaining by all lawful means conditions and developments in the receiving state, and promoting friendly relations.

But with revolutionary changes in communications and transportation and the proliferation of diplomatic summits, many began to question the need for ambassadors and the diplomatic establishments they presided over. George Ball, a senior State Department official in the Kennedy and Johnson administrations,

Jan and Kerstin Eliasson with George and Laura Bush

famously declined an offer by President Jimmy Carter to be an ambassador, saying he had no desire to be "an innkeeper for visiting Congressmen."

Henry Kissinger offered his own withering assessment when he declared that "ambassadors don't count anymore." He twisted the knife further when he said that ambassadors are "nothing more than lackeys."

Zbigniew Brzezinski, Carter's national security adviser, dismissed modern embassies and diplomatic structures as "a boondoggle and waste of time. For the most part," Brzezinski said, "serious business is not conducted by the ambassador. In my time, there were about a dozen ambassadors with whom I had worthwhile exchanges and learned a good deal. But usually, it's just an exhausting exercise and a waste of time."

ৡ III ৡ

Ridiculed and dismissed, ambassadors began to fight back in the way they know best: they commissioned reports. In 1983, "The Modern Ambassador: The Challenge and the Search," edited by Martin F. Herz of the Institute for the Study of Diplomacy in Washington, DC, insisted on the need for, and continuing relevance of, ambassadors. The study acknowledged that many believed the resident mission presided over by an ambassador was increasingly archaic and ineffectual. It conceded that advances in technology, communications, and international travel made it easier for government officials to conduct business directly with their overseas counterparts. Additionally, it noted that many leaders were convinced that representation and negotiation are done most effectively by direct contacts between high level officials, thus obviating the need for an ambassador.

But the institute report concluded that while ambassadors have been deprived of traditional functions, there was little to be gained by lamenting this; it was much wiser to focus on the steady expansion of the ambassador's functions into other areas. The report said the new ambassadorial role was a significant one that included management, politics, public education, cultural relations, trade, and development economics.

Another report, commissioned fifteen years later by the American Academy of Diplomacy, also asserted that ambassadors are crucial to the advancement of a nation's foreign policy. Ambassadors, it said, are the first line of defense for a country.

But some critics continue to question the efficacy of ambassadors and the diplomatic establishments they preside over. Shaun Riordan, a former British diplomat, argues that ambassadors are no longer competent to deal with complex international issues. The scope and complexity of issues such as terrorism, human rights, environment, trade, health, and migration require that nations dispatch technical experts to negotiate with each other.

"The traditional model of generalist career diplomats, who in principal can operate in any area of work, is no longer viable," he writes in his 2003 book, *The New Diplomacy.* He adds that the cost of brick-and-mortar diplomatic establishments is largely a waste and that scarce resources should be used for other purposes.

❦ IV ❦

Most diplomatic experts and practitioners say the job of ambassador is not irrelevant, but it is changing. G. R. Berridge, a British scholar, says that modern diplomats are involved marginally in negotiation, but play critical roles in information gathering, lobbying, clarifying intentions, supporting commercial and financial activities, assisting nationals abroad, and promoting popular sympathy for their nation's foreign policy.

"So the resident embassy, concerning which obituaries have been written in the 70s and 80s, is still alive," Berridge writes in his 2002 book, *Diplomacy: Theory and Practice.*

Kishan S. Rana, a former diplomat in India, has also written extensively on the role of ambassadors and the embassies they now preside over. His book *The 21st-Century Ambassador* makes a compelling case for the continued relevance of ambassadors. Rana argues that the role of the ambassador has changed markedly from the classical era in which envoys served as conduits of information from their own prince or president to the leaders of the country they were appointed to. But he is convinced that embassies are now more important than ever and that ambassadors who are creative and innovative can play a pivotal role in advancing their countries' interests.

To do so, ambassadors should recognize that revolutions in transportation and communication have fundamentally changed their jobs. But rather than lament the loss of certain powers and responsibilities, they should seize on the opportunity to be more relevant in other areas. The modern ambassador surely does not determine war and peace between states, but plays an important role in reducing tensions and developing relationships. Rana argues that in the entire government, ambassadors are the ones who have the best overview, in real time, of the current shape and content of the bilateral relationship entrusted to their charge. This produces an opportunity for bargaining, linkage, and tradeoffs, across the full range of issues in which the countries are engaged.

So rather than comparing modern ambassadors to mythical envoys who could decide war and peace, it is more helpful to think of them as the chief executive of a country unit of a transnational enterprise. Like corporate leaders, the ambassador knows the local scene, has authority over the embassy, and is positioned to function as the best adviser to headquarters.

The ambassador's true value is that of a principal advisor on the overall policy that applies to the country where he or she is based, within the framework of headquarters' vision and strategy. The ambassador also executes approved policy on the ground and manages the delivery process, and is held accountable for results. The corporate analogy, Rana says, may take some of the mystique out of the ambassador's work but it directs attention to his chief tasks.

The first is negotiation. While modern ambassadors dealing in bilateral (or country-to-country) diplomacy are less involved in conducting formal negotiations than their predecessors, this is still part of the job. For the most part, countries have moved from classic political negotiations to a search for agreement in narrow, specialized functional areas. For example, two countries' departments of transportation are involved in highly technical negotiations on a civil aviation protocol. The agencies send technical specialists from home, and the ambassador's role is limited. When the specialist teams from home arrive, the ambassador typically assigns one of the embassy's economic or commercial counselors to monitor the talks and help out when needed. The ambassador might offer a broad political and economic briefing for the team upon its arrival, receive progress reports as the talks unfold, offer advice if blockages develop, and try to knock down any obstacles that may arise.

The second main area of responsibility for a modern ambassador is promotion. This refers to the ambassador's work to articulate his country's views or interests in all areas: politics, economics, culture, education, science and technology, information and media, even consular affairs. In the promotional area, the envoy essentially works on his personal initiative rather than under a set of instructions. Promotion is most typically thought of in the context of articulating broad political views, but it has increasingly begun to include economics.

Rana argues that after political work, economic diplomacy is usually the ambassador's second priority. This includes promotion of trade, investments, aid and technical cooperation, image building, and tourism. Ambassadors are their country's first salesman in their host country.

Related to promotion is outreach or relationship building by ambassadors and their team, aimed at both traditional and untraditional local partners.

The fourth area is feedback. This refers to the ambassador's responsibility to report back home what is going on in the host country. The ambassador needs to go beyond the recitation of headlines that can be followed closely enough through CNN, *the Economist, New York Times,* and other news organizations. The ambassador adds value by offering analysis, perspective, and forward-leaning assessments that are oriented to policy or tactical recommendations.

The fifth area of ambassadorial responsibility is management. This includes the day-to-day tactical management of the broad relationship with the host nation, fulfilling the performance objectives set by the government at home, and overseeing the internal functioning of the embassy, including its resources.

The final area is servicing. This refers to those initiatives that bring the embassy into contact with the public, such as consular work.

Rana argues that for ambassadors to be successful, they should possess certain skills. These include a broad-ranging knowledge and curiosity, a solid understanding about what is going on at home, a strong grasp of national and global economics, a polished media presence, innovative thinking skills, a fascination with international relations, and a command of at least one major language other than one's native tongue.

Ambassadors, he argues, must work diligently in their host country while staying plugged in at home. "That the home base has become so important is also a change from the past," he said. The modern ambassador, Rana says, should be skilled at working with the host government, speaking to the general public, and interacting with specialists in areas ranging from science and technology, to culture, politics, and economics. This demands an ability to master diversity and complexity.

Rana notes that in earlier diplomatic eras, ambassadors enjoyed direct access to leaders and heads of state and didn't get involved in trade, investment, culture, science, and the media. But the ambassador is now more involved in so-called low diplomacy, which includes work on trade, investment, technology, health, and education matters.

While this seems unglamorous, it represents the essence of contemporary international life. Ambassadors must handle details, master logistics, remove obstacles, and follow up on projects. And much of their power is what has been called soft power—the power to persuade, the ability to get what you want through attraction rather than coercion or force.

CHAPTER 3

The Ambassador from Central Casting

Jan and Kerstin Eliasson

๛ I ๛

On January 17, 1995, Jan Eliasson, then Sweden's deputy foreign minister, went to the Swedish parliament for an auspicious occasion: to give a speech to commemorate the fiftieth anniversary of the disappearance of Raoul Wallenberg. It was an important event to celebrate one of Sweden's national icons. As one of Sweden's top diplomats, Eliasson became fascinated with the life and legacy of Wallenberg, and as part of a high-level task force had carefully studied the Swedish archives to understand Wallenberg's life and tragic disappearance, presumably in a Soviet prison camp.

Eliasson used his speech before the parliament to lavish praise on the heroism of one Swede and to identify Wallenberg's valor with the aspirations of the entire nation. His speech was also personally revealing, illustrating the passions Eliasson had acquired in his first three decades as a diplomat and foreshadowing themes that would dominate his final decade as a Swedish envoy.

Raoul Wallenberg, Eliasson told the lawmakers, acted bravely and boldly in the summer of 1944 when he traveled to Budapest and risked his life so he could save as many as he could of the two hundred thousand Jews who still remained in Hungary after the death and deportation of more than six hundred thousand.

"I am sure that in these situations he thought of the danger of delay, the damage caused by waiting too long and not acting in time, of being forced to focus on putting out the cruel flames instead of looking for arsonists and the causes of fire. Arriving in time, to forestall and take preventive action, is basically a question of respect for life and respect for human dignity," Eliasson said, using Wallenberg's life to underscore his conviction about the need for leaders and governments to act early in crises to prevent violence and suffering. Eliasson observed that Wallenberg, the scion of a wealthy Stockholm family, could have enjoyed a life of comfort, even luxury, but decided to put all of that at risk in the pursuit of a higher calling when he traveled to Hungary.

"He was one of us, a man who showed that action is possible and necessary. He showed that we do not always need to be prepared or to take deliberate actions to do what is right. He showed that we all can rise to the occasion, which then can take over and inspire us to a superhuman effort," Eliasson said.

In celebrating the legacy of Wallenberg, Eliasson cited his favorite quote from Bertrand Russell, one of his favorite authors. While Eliasson said the words referred to Wallenberg, they shed as much insight into the mind and heart of Jan Eliasson. Quoting Russell, he said:

> Three passions, simple but overwhelmingly strong, have governed my life: the longing for love, the search for knowledge, and unbearable pity for the suffering of mankind. These passions, like great winds, have blown me hither and thither, in a wayward course, over a deep ocean of anguish, reaching to the very verge of despair.

ৡ **II** ৡ

Jan Eliasson was born in Gothenburg, on the west coast of Sweden, in 1940. The son of a metalworker and a seamstress, he was an athletic and academically gifted boy who loved reading and sports.

"I was at the top of the class. I was a good athlete. Football was my game," he recalled. Eliasson was also inquisitive and loved to learn. "I read a lot. I almost destroyed my eyes," he said, adding that he used a flashlight to read at night under his sheets. He had a close relationship with both of his parents, and their influence continued in his life. "If your father was a metalworker and your mother was a seamstress you recognize your parents in everybody," he said.

Eliasson said his father was a prominent member of his community, an active, forceful, but modest man. "He was a real leader. He earned tremendous respect everywhere. He always wanted me to be a politician."

Jan has a younger brother, Roger Holtback, who is a successful businessman in Sweden. The two are separated by more than four years and have a relationship that is both cordial and competitive.

"We had the advantage of extremely good parents," Roger says. "You couldn't ask for better parents. They were supportive, open-minded, and highly respected in the community. They taught us to work hard, to be outgoing, to be responsible. They were very good examples of how to live."

Roger recalls his older brother as a hard worker who also had an easy and enjoyable personality.

"Jan was an extremely good student, one of the top students in Sweden for his age. He worked very hard, but he was so interested in his studies. He was also a good athlete. He was a fun, very likeable guy."

As a high school student Eliasson was selected to participate in an overseas exchange program and spent the 1957–58 academic year in Decatur, Indiana. It was a time that was hugely important for Eliasson, as he developed a lifelong love of politics and travel and a fascination with the United States. During his subsequent professional years in the United States, he referred often to his grounding in the American Midwest, noting that he graduated from an American high school before he graduated from his Swedish high school.

His American father was active in local Democratic politics. Jan helped his "dad" arrange the annual Democratic fund-raising dinner and suggested he choose a young senator from Massachusetts to speak at the dinner—John F. Kennedy—rather than the more obvious candidate, Tennessee Senator

Estes Kefauver, who had been the 1956 Democratic vice presidential nominee. During the dinner Eliasson was called to the front of the room and received a handshake from Kennedy. Nearly a half century later, Eliasson tells the story with such vividness that you would swear it took place yesterday.

Eliasson returned home and attended the Swedish Naval Academy, where he graduated in 1962. "I had a strong sense of discovery, to see new horizons. I wanted some fresh air," he said of his decision to join the navy. Eliasson often refers to his naval experiences to describe disparate things: his love of the sea, his ability to run things with a stern hand if necessary, and his preference to work in an environment in which all are content.

"I'm a naval officer. I've been on a happy ship and I've been on an unhappy ship. I prefer being on a happy ship," he said, summarizing his management philosophy.

Eliasson earned a master's degree in economics in 1965. That year he decided to take the entrance exam to join Sweden's prestigious foreign service. He was one of fifteen invited to join the diplomatic corps. He entered on September 20, 1965.

"We were very spoiled to have this very good program," he said. This involved a one-year stint in various sections of the foreign ministry—four months in the political section, four months in the trade department, and four months in the consulate section. Eliasson's second year of diplomatic training consisted of a half year in the Finance Ministry and a half year at the Organization of Economic Cooperation and Development in Paris.

Of Eliasson's class of fifteen diplomats, about half became ambassadors, and almost all became lifelong friends. "There was a tremendous sense of solidarity," he said.

Tapped early on as a star and as a potential ambassador, Eliasson won important postings to Bonn, Washington, and Salisbury in Zimbabwe, where he opened the first Swedish embassy in 1980. He was the first secretary in the Swedish embassy in Washington in the 1970s, a time when his government was often at odds with the Nixon administration. He still speaks sarcastically about working in Washington during the "joyful days of the 1970s" when disagreements over Vietnam and arms-control strategy divided Europeans and Americans. As the result of some bitter exchanges between Swedish leaders and the Nixon administration, the United States declined to accept a Swedish ambassador in Washington for more than a year and withdrew the American ambassador in Stockholm.

Eliasson's stint in Washington was deeply stimulating and fueled his ambition to return as head of the embassy. He recalls sitting in the ambassador's elegant Nebraska Avenue residence and deciding he wanted to come back some day—as the occupant of the house.

"I think I wanted to be the ambassador," he says with a smile.

৵ III ৵

Eliasson served as the diplomatic adviser to the Swedish prime minister, Olof Palme, from 1982 to 1983 and then as the director general for political affairs in the Ministry of Foreign Affairs from 1983 to 1987. Palme was an important mentor for Eliasson and they worked together closely on a number of projects, including a grueling effort to end the Iran-Iraq war, representing the UN.

"Palme was very important. He was a giant in Sweden. He was extremely colorful. I was very close to him," Eliasson said. Palme was a dominant figure in Swedish politics for more than two decades. While coming from an upper-class background, he was an active member of the Social Democratic Party that has dominated Swedish politics for the past seventy-five years.

An aide to Prime Minister Tage Erlander, Palme became interested in international development cooperation, nuclear disarmament, and European unification. He strongly supported a powerful defense establishment to ensure Sweden's neutrality, a policy that was defined as nonparticipation in alliances in peacetime and neutrality in time of war.

Palme entered the cabinet in 1963 as a minister without portfolio and then took a succession of cabinet posts until in 1969 he succeeded Erlander as party chairman and then prime minister. Palme served as prime minister from 1969 to 1976, then the opposition leader from 1976 to 1982, and then again as prime minister from 1982 to his death in 1986.

Eliasson said Palme was an inspiring, hard-driving, workaholic with a clear vision of the world and a combative approach to politics. He drove his young aide hard.

"He called me at all hours. Thankfully, most of the time I was one step ahead of him in the reading."

Photographs of Eliasson from that time show a very lean, highly intense young man. Eliasson's collaboration with Palme has caused him to reflect on working styles. Palme could be tough and combative and contentious. Eliasson said the approach worked well for Palme, but was never his preferred way of operating. He cited one of Aesop's Fables involving a contest between the sun and the wind as to which was stronger. They agreed to settle the dispute by holding a contest to see which could make a traveler take off his coat first. The wind blew with all its might and stirred up a blast of frigid air.

But the traveler only clutched his jacket tighter. Then the sun went to work: the rays of sunshine and warmth compelled the traveler to take off his coat. The sun was declared the winner and ever since persuasion has been held in higher esteem than force.

"Indeed, sunshine of a kind and gentle manner will sooner open a poor man's heart than all the threats and force of blustering authority," the fable concludes.

"I think the sun method is most effective to get the result," Eliasson said.

If persuasion is a central feature of Eliasson's diplomatic style, so is tenacity. At one point in the 1980s, Sweden was given the opportunity to mediate the drafting of a constitution in Guatemala between the government and a rebel group. Eliasson was seen as one of the foreign ministry's top mediators, but was not fully fluent in Spanish. Determined to be part of the mediation team, Eliasson took a ten-day Spanish immersion course that was offered in a monastery school in Antigua. He improved his Spanish and used the classes to "more or less play out the negotiations." Eliasson then took part in the mediation, conducting the negotiations for two and a half hours in Spanish.

"I had the most horrible headache after that. But everybody was impressed that I was able to use my Spanish," Eliasson recalled.

He also remembered helping draft a report to Stockholm reporting on what had happened. He insisted the report describe the complexity of the talks—and noted they were conducted in Spanish.

৯৯ IV ৯৯

After Palme was assassinated in 1986 Eliasson was deeply distraught, but continued the Iran-Iraq mediation effort under the auspices of the United Nations. Eliasson made more than twenty visits to the two countries in the 1980s and early 1990s. He spent twenty-five hours in negotiations with Saddam Hussein, probably more than any living Western diplomat.

He said his visits to Saddam's presidential palaces reminded him of the Charlie Chaplin movie, *The Great Dictator*. "As you walked through the palace, you were supposed to feel smaller and smaller, weaker and weaker," he recalled. "People were really scared. The guards were terrified. In those rooms, you could almost cut the fear with a knife." He recalls Saddam as "arrogant and haughty. He was very focused. He was very concentrated. He looked you straight in the eye. He made you uncomfortable."

Later, Eliasson warned Iraq's Foreign Minister Tariq Aziz about the threat posed by Iran's human waves unless an agreement was reached. "Aziz said, we don't care. We have the ultimate weapons," the ambassador recalls, an apparent reference to chemical and biological weapons. In 1981, Saddam declined a truce with Iran that he largely accepted near the end of the decade, after hundreds of thousands of young Iranians and Iraqis had lost their lives and billions of dollars in Iraqi and Iranian national treasuries had been squandered.

"In mediation you have to find that moment when both sides are equally strong or equally weak," Eliasson said, adding that the difficulty in mediating the Iraq-Iran war was that the power balance kept shifting.

Eliasson's experiences with Saddam left him with a strong dislike of the dictator, but also with frustration that global leaders left him in place to brutalize his own people. They were content to impose sanctions on his country that did little to hurt Saddam, but resulted in horrible suffering for many Iraqis.

"I'm very critical of sanctions that are not precise or targeted," Eliasson said. "It's sad the focus had to change from getting rid of one of the worst dictators in the world to getting rid of his weapons of mass destruction. You can't go to the UN to get rid of Hitler. This is the moral dilemma: you don't go to the UN for regime change, only technical issues such as getting rid of WMD," he said.

Eliasson was Sweden's ambassador to the United Nations from 1988 to 1992. He also served as the UN secretary general's personal representative on the Iran and Iraq conflict during this time. He chaired the UN General Assembly's working group on emergency relief in 1991 and played an important role in negotiating the creation of a new UN office of humanitarian affairs.

A Swedish journalist who covered Eliasson during his UN years said the ambassador was completely in his element. "Jan knew everybody, grabbed everyone's hand as he walked through the corridors. He excels in person-to-person diplomacy. He's a star."

In 1992, Eliasson was selected as the United Nation's first undersecretary-general for humanitarian affairs, a job that took him to such grim places as Somalia, Sudan, Mozambique, and the Balkans. This experience fueled his passion for humanitarian actions to help peoples and countries in need. He said the debacle in Somalia haunted him for years and continues to inspire him about the wisdom of preventive diplomacy.

His work to provide relief to Sudan also reminded him that diplomacy, when done well and creatively, can be a force for good. He recalls that efforts to get emergency assistance in that war-ravaged nation were stalled because of the unwillingness of the warring parties to agree on a cease-fire. For the government, negotiating a cease-fire was seen as giving the rebel forces legitimacy. One of Eliasson's aides suggested that the idea should be repackaged as the establishment of humanitarian corridors. The parties agreed to this, allowing for the safe passage of emergency aid that ended up saving thousands of people.

"Careful and creative language is important in diplomacy," Eliasson said.

 formula V formula

In 1994, in a clear indication that he had reached the top tier of Swedish diplomacy, Eliasson was appointed deputy foreign minister, the second most important job in Swedish diplomacy and the top job for career diplomats. For six years he was near the pinnacle of Swedish diplomacy, charged to formulate policy and run the foreign service bureaucracy.

As deputy foreign minister, he managed more than eighteen hundred diplomats and staffers. Swedish journalists who observed Eliasson during this period say he was a creative diplomat who was superb at explaining Swedish foreign policy to the public, but was less successful as an administrator.

"Jan is much better with people than with his papers," a Swedish diplomat told me.

Eliasson worked under Foreign Minister Lena Hjelm-Wallen and then Anna Lindh, who became the foreign minister in 1998 after serving as the minister of the environment. With both foreign ministers Eliasson reviewed Sweden's policies on a wide range of issues including Swedish security policy, UN peacekeeping, European Union enlargement, Baltic Sea cooperation, European relations with Islam, human rights, international law, and deepening contacts with the nongovernmental organization (NGO) community.

Eliasson oversaw an ambitious effort to draft a white paper on how the international community could prevent future humanitarian disasters. His UN experiences had seared in his mind the need to develop stronger preventive policies. During a sabbatical year in 1994, Eliasson worked on prevention strategies with Peter Wallensteen from the Department of Peace and Conflict Resolution at Sweden's Uppsala University.

Eliasson developed a so-called ladder of prevention that comprises steps that can be taken to prevent humanitarian disasters. These steps include early warning systems to detect potential disasters, fact-finding missions, mediation, and arbitration. Additional steps include the preventive deployment of troops or observers and what are called Chapter 7 measures—smart sanctions and the credible threat of force or use of force.

In a later refinement of the paradigm, Eliasson outlined a number of steps to take after force was used to avoid the recurrence of military conflict. These include humanitarian programs, peacekeeping, building democratic institutions and civil society, reconstruction and development programs, and measures to help reconciliation between the disputing parties. Eliasson believes this pyramid of prevention offers concrete steps that can be taken by parties to a possible conflict, as well as other governments, international organizations, and NGOs.

After eight months of intense work, Eliasson helped prepare a plan to deal with both the root causes of conflict (structural prevention) and direct measures to stop conflict from turning violent or reoccurring (operational prevention). The goal was to create a culture of prevention.

The Swedish government realized that its program of prevention, which was released in 1999, would have little impact if it was pushed by Sweden alone. Lindh decided to put the prevention agenda at the top of the European Union's agenda when Sweden held the rotating EU presidency in the first half of 2001. The European Union adopted a program for the Prevention of Violent Conflict in Gothenburg in June 2001 that set the political priorities for preventive actions and identified the European Union's instruments for long- and short-term prevention.

❧ VI ❧

After six years as deputy foreign minister, Eliasson felt it was time to move on. Some Swedish diplomats say Lindh also wanted a deputy who was more a tidy manager and less a forceful public personality than Eliasson. An intriguing option for Eliasson appeared in 2000 as Sweden's ambassador to the United States, Rolf Ekeus, prepared to retire. Eliasson and his wife, Kerstin, love Washington and jumped at the chance to represent their country in the political capital of the world.

"I saw this was my chance. Rolf Ekeus was going to retire. We love the atmosphere in Washington. We feel comfortable here. We feel so much at home here. This was a step down. I jokingly said I have to get used to receiving rather than giving instructions," Eliasson said.

Before moving to Washington in September of 2000, Eliasson took his customary summer vacation in the family's summer home in Gotland, an island on the Baltic Sea. He used the time to relax with his family, work outdoors, and plan for his return to Washington. Eliasson drafted some preliminary ideas on how he wanted to approach the job.

He identified communities and institutions that he wanted to develop high-level access to including the Clinton administration, the Bush and Gore campaigns, the State Department, Congress, the media, the think tank world, and the Swedish American community. Eliasson reviewed the high-level contacts with American officials he had developed over his long diplomatic career and the friends and acquaintances he had made during his work in Washington in the 1970s and in New York from 1988 to 1994. His primary focus was to use his personal American contacts and those of his predecessor to develop a high-level network in Washington.

This network would allow him to anticipate any problems in the bilateral relationship between the United States and Sweden—and solve them before they grew serious. The network would also allow him opportunities to present Sweden's view of the world in Washington. When Eliasson arrived in Washington in the late summer of 2000 he was determined to use his experience and contacts to advance Sweden's agenda in the political capital of the world.

"I can have a lot of influence in Sweden or a little influence in the U.S.—now I'm ready to have a little influence in Washington," he recalls thinking as he prepared to come to Washington.

❧ VII ❧

Eliasson brought to Washington some strong views about diplomacy and a diplomatic style that had evolved over four decades. Above all, the ambassador brought a love for his work that is undiminished.

"I have great respect for diplomacy, for the art of diplomacy. I have my personal views, but I have always tried to be a diplomat—to stand up for the tradition of Swedish diplomacy. I love the work. I love the trade. It's the most civilized way to solve conflicts."

Eliasson has a diplomatic style that was rooted in his nation's traditions but also very specific to him. A classically trained European diplomat, Eliasson was experienced in bilateral as well as multilateral diplomacy, such as that conducted at the United Nations. The most noticeable aspect of his diplomatic style is his energy and passion. He loves the intricate chess game of what it takes to influence decisions. He is fascinated by institutions and has a shrewd understanding of how decisions are made and how power flows in government.

Friendly and outgoing, he has an ease with people that is striking in the United States and almost stunning in Sweden.

"Jan is a remarkably charming person with very good people skills. If you go to a reception at his embassy and he's in a room with one hundred people he knows everyone's names," said Chester Crocker, a former American diplomat and now a professor at Georgetown University.

Anders Hellner, an analyst at the Swedish Institute for International Affairs in Stockholm, said Eliasson's personal skills have been a trademark of his career: "Swedes never remember anyone's first name; Jan remembers everyone's first name. He's much more American in that respect. When he walks into a room he talks to everyone. He's very outgoing and friendly to everyone, even people he doesn't know that well. He remembers everyone."

A second aspect of Eliasson's diplomatic style is an attention to detail. He is convinced that small gestures count, especially in diplomacy. For example, in 2004 he made a special effort to attend the confirmation hearing of President George W. Bush's nominee as American ambassador in Stockholm, Teel Bivins. At that same hearing several other nominees were considered for diplomatic posts, but no other ambassador attended.

"I thought it was a matter of courtesy," Eliasson said.

Ambitious and driven, Eliasson also has a light touch. He knows when to push and when to pull back and wait. For example, a few years ago he saw Condoleezza Rice at a Supreme Court concert in which she was performing on the piano, as was Kerstin Eliasson, also a fine pianist. Rice was then the National Security Council (NSC) advisor and Eliasson wanted to discuss a few matters. He saw her before her piano performance, but could tell she was anxious. So he bantered with her lightly, wished her well, and then sought her out after her performance—to congratulate her and to transact his business.

"When you talk to people, under what circumstances is very important in diplomacy. Timing is so important," he said.

Eliasson's style and professionalism impressed the right people in Stockholm and in Washington. Richard Lugar, the chairman of the Senate Foreign Relations Committee, said Eliasson is a diplomat whom he takes very seriously: "The ambassador is one of the really excellent diplomats in this city. He has an impressive, wide-ranging background and comes from a country with a remarkable tradition in diplomacy and international affairs," Lugar said.

Paul Sarbanes, the Democratic senator from Maryland who is a senior member of the foreign relations panel, is a huge fan of the ambassador. "He's one of the most extraordinary diplomats I've ever come across in Washington and I come across most of them. He's highly intelligent, utterly charming, very experienced, and very substantive. He understands the United States and is held in very high regard in Sweden. He has such a warm, disarming personality that it increases his professional effectiveness," Sarbanes said.

"There are ambassadors and then there are ambassadors," said Walter Cutler, president of Meridian International and a former U.S. ambassador to Saudi Arabia. "Jan is one of the most active and highly regarded ambassadors in this city and he does it without the advantage of representing a great power. The real test of an ambassador's diplomatic skill is to be taken seriously and viewed as influential when you come from a small country," Cutler said. "He has tremendous experience, a wonderfully outgoing personality, is as sharp as a tack, listens well, has a great sense of humor, and a delightful and impressive wife. You can tell how successful he is by the people you see at his residence. Everyone wants to go the Swedish residence."

Eliasson is well regarded back home—a fact that was noted in Washington. Hans Dahlgren, Sweden's deputy foreign minister, told me that Eliasson is one of Sweden's best diplomats: "Jan Eliasson is a unique Swedish diplomat. He has wider experience than anyone you could find in our system today. He has worked both bilaterally and multilaterally. He has worked within the UN system as undersecretary general for humanitarian affairs. He has worked closely with Olof Palme, mediating in between Iran and Iraq. He is a very good communicator. He can explain difficult international issues to a television audience. Not every diplomat has that communication skill."

Urban Ahlin, chairman of the Swedish parliament's Foreign Relations Committee, said Eliasson is admired across Sweden's political spectrum: "He has a long career in diplomatic service and a very positive reputation from left to right. He's an enormously likable guy. It's rare that you meet someone with that kind of social capability he has," Ahlin said.

"Jan Eliasson tries to bring his old traditional ways of thinking—his contacts with Palme, his work on Iran and Iraq, his mediation. But at the same time he's modern, in line with what is happening today. He comes from the Old World and can explain the New World as well," he added.

Gunilla Carlson, deputy chairman of the Swedish parliament's Foreign Affairs Committee, said Eliasson is open, accessible, and charming: "I admire him as a person and a professional. He uses his personality in a professional way. He is willing to listen and learn. He is always in control of himself. He makes people feel very comfortable, He's well prepared. He is a crown jewel of Swedish diplomacy. He's not a central figure in Swedish policy making. But he's still the star when it comes to diplomacy. A new generation of young diplomats look up to him and see how hard he works. He works day and night," she said.

Per Ahlin, the foreign editor of *Dagens Nyheter,* a leading Stockholm daily newspaper, said Eliasson has an openness that is unusual among

Swedish diplomats. "When he was the deputy foreign minister, he opened up the foreign ministry completely. He was a person who was present in the foreign policy debate. He was really open and really visible. He did a lot of good for Swedish foreign policy." Ahlin said Eliasson is a polished and persuasive voice on Swedish television.

"He's a diplomat saying that diplomacy is not standing under a chandelier sipping wine and eating shrimp in some fancy environment. It's sitting in a small office with no windows, working really long hours with boring meetings, drinking coffee out of plastic mugs. He takes some of the aura out of diplomacy and describes it as hard work. He often says that diplomacy is not what you think."

The ambassador has critics. One Swedish diplomat who has known Eliasson for years said he can be friendly, caring, and show genuine empathy but is also deeply ambitious, competitive, and self-promotional.

"He has built much of his career on using his charm and working-class origin to ingratiate himself with the Social Democratic prime and foreign ministers. His driving forces have always been his determination to get to the top no matter what."

In reflecting back over his forty-year career in diplomacy, Eliasson said his wife Kerstin played a critical role in supporting his professional aspirations, taking the lead role in raising their three children, and pursuing her own career as one of Europe's most respected experts in science policy.

Kerstin Eliasson has an undergraduate degree in French from Stockholm University and a master's degree in sociology from American University. Kerstin worked in Stockholm and during her husband's postings to New York and Washington. She served as director of research policy in the Swedish Ministry of Education and Science and chaired the science committee of the Organisation for Economic Co-operation and Development (OECD).

When the Eliassons came to Washington in 2000, Kerstin was the science counselor in the embassy. She left Washington in February 2004 to become the deputy minister of education in Stockholm.

"She is one of Europe's foremost experts on science policy. On a personal level, I don't think I would be here without her. She's given me stability and joy. I'm enormously proud of her. Her new job gives us an equality professionally that is stimulating personally," the ambassador says. "The offer to go back to Stockholm and work in the government came as a mixed blessing. She loved her life in Washington," he said.

The Eliassons have three children, Anna, Emilie, and Johan, and five grandchildren.

CHAPTER 4

Sweden's Washington Agenda

Eliasson at a staff meeting with Sweden's defense minister, Leni Bjorklund

༜ I ༜

Jan Eliasson, like his Swedish diplomatic predecessors, came to Washington to do several basic but ambitious things: to offer a narrative of the Swedish American relationship, to present an image of Sweden as a vibrant and active country, to outline Sweden's vision of the world, and to address any bilateral problems between Sweden and the United States.

Ambassadors explain and defend their nation's policies, they don't create them. Eliasson as a senior diplomat had flexibility to focus on issues and themes that he felt appropriate, but he was given a brief to implement. During his time in Washington, Eliasson emphasized Sweden's long relationship with the United States and tended to describe it as an unbroken run of tranquility except for a difficult stretch in the 1970s.

The ambassador noted that Sweden has one of the oldest diplomatic relationships with the United States of any country in the world. He and other Swedish diplomats often remind listeners that Benjamin Franklin and Gustav Philip Creutz signed the Treaty of Amity and Commerce in Paris in 1783, confirming that a relationship between the two countries already existed. But Eliasson was fond of saying that Sweden's connection to the United States predated even the signing of that treaty. He was very interested in the Swedish colony of New Sweden that was established in the Delaware valley in 1638. This colony underscored Sweden's early connection to the United States.

Eliasson often discussed Swedish immigration to the United States, saluting the bravery of the Swedes who left their homes and noting their contribution to American life. In the mid-1800s, emigration from Sweden to the United States was widespread. Fleeing hunger and poverty and seeking a better life, more than one million Swedes migrated to the United States. While not as ubiquitous as the Irish or Italians or Germans, Swedish immigrants were an important part of the American experience, especially in the upper Midwest. As recently as 1930, Chicago was home to more Swedes than any city other than Stockholm, Gothenburg, and Malmo. In his talks, especially to Swedish American groups, Eliasson would note the enormous difficulty of the immigrant experience for Swedes in the United States. But he would add that their contributions were important to their adopted nation.

Eliasson often noted the difficult period of American Swedish relations during the 1970s, but did so in an easy, self-deprecating way. Eliasson was a diplomat at the Swedish embassy in Washington at the time. Interestingly, Eliasson, who has been a strong proponent of closer ties between the United States and Sweden, worked under the man—Olof Palme—who tossed this relationship into great turmoil.

Palme, as an education minister in 1968, led a torchlight parade in Stockholm with the North Vietnamese ambassador to the Soviet Union. In 1970, Palme visited the United States without an invitation, the first head of government to do so without meeting the president since Fidel Castro came to the United Nations in 1959. In late 1972, the United States withdrew its ambassador from Stockholm. When Palme compared the American bombings of Vietnam to Nazi extermination camps, Henry Kissinger and Richard Nixon decided to put American relations with Sweden into a deep freeze that lasted for almost two years. They are now referred to in Sweden as the "years of frost."

Swedish American relations were complex during the Cold War. Swedish leaders often pushed an arms control and disarmament agenda that varied sharply from American policy. Sweden's active support of tough environmental policy was sometimes dismissed in the United States as utopian and impractical for a major industrial power.

Eliasson, as diplomats are trained to do, focused on the positive nature of America's relationship with Sweden. He focused on shared values and intermingled blood as signs of a close bond between the two nations.

❧ II ❧

In addition to emphasizing the historic links between the United States and Sweden, Eliasson was careful to describe Sweden as an attractive, efficient, consequential, and active country—despite its own imperfections. Sweden's Washington embassy distributed a raft of materials that portrayed Sweden as a successful society that is also wrestling with problems that confront other nations such as immigration and racial integration. Embassy literature depicted Sweden as an environmentally friendly, physically beautiful nation committed to transparency and openness. Sweden, the ambassador emphasized, is the home to innovative twenty-first-century companies that are globally competitive in such sectors as information technology, telecommunications, biomedicine, medical research, and design.

The literature argues that Sweden's evolution from a poor, backward, agrarian country to a modern, industrial nation in the space of only half a century is an economic miracle comparable to Japan. Eliasson frequently described Sweden as a medium-sized nation located in an increasingly important place in Europe: northern Europe. While home to only nine million people, Sweden, he noted, is one of Europe's largest nations geographically, about the size of Spain or France or California.

The ambassador acknowledged that Sweden's approach to government is different from that of the United States. Swedes are accustomed to paying more in taxes but expect more in government services in areas ranging from health to education to child care and elder care. Eliasson went out of his way to describe Sweden as a nation that takes its global responsibilities seriously, whether it be in peacekeeping or economic development. Eliasson developed a list of specific

Swedish activities that included its participation in training Iraqi troops, dispatching peacekeepers to the Balkans, helping rebuild Afghanistan, and offering generous amounts of development assistance.

"Sweden is an active country," he said repeatedly.

☺ III ☺

In addition to sketching a view of Sweden as an attractive and vibrant society, Eliasson argued that Sweden is committed to being a constructive and engaged member of the global community. Eliasson said it was in Sweden's enlightened self-interest to be a participant in the world, working with its Baltic and Nordic neighbors and contributing to reforms in the European Union and the United Nations. Eliasson and other Swedish diplomats argued that the new world of globalization shows that artificial divisions between nations are less relevant than before.

Natural disasters and environmental degradation, poverty and pandemics, terrorism and organized crime, failing states and regional conflicts, war and weapons of mass destruction, all these are threats to every country, Swedish Foreign Minister Laila Freivalds said when she outlined Sweden's foreign policy agenda in 2005. Swedish diplomats advocate a world in which international law is an important and respected force for good. They argue that a system of global rules brings about fairness and security, especially for small and medium-sized nations.

The United Nations, Swedish diplomats say, is the cornerstone of their country's foreign and security policy. The United Nations has been important to Sweden since it joined the world body in 1946. One of Sweden's most distinguished public servants, Dag Hammarskjöld, was the second secretary general of the United Nations and arguably one of the giants in UN history. Swedes argue that while large countries may not realize they need the United Nations, smaller nations know they do for protection and as a forum to express their views. Swedish leaders say that working closely with and in the United Nations is the best way to influence the global system and make contributions. Eliasson frequently noted that more than eighty thousand Swedes have taken part in UN peacekeeping operations over the years. Sweden uses the United Nations as an important channel for its contributions to development assistance.

Year after year, Sweden is one of the world's most generous contributors to development assistance relative to the size of its economy. In a Commitment to Development Index designed by the Center for Global Development, a respected think tank, to rank the generosity of twenty-one rich nations on how they help or hinder the poor, in 2005 Sweden ranked third, behind only Denmark and the Netherlands. The index ranked the nations based on seven areas of government policy: foreign aid, trade, investment, migration, environment, security, and technology.

Eliasson frequently argued that Sweden was determined to be a strong leader in northern Europe and was committed to helping make the Baltic Sea region an engine of peace and prosperity in northern Europe. Eliasson and other Swedish diplomats also emphasize their strong support for the European Union's efforts to develop a closer and stronger community, adding that the European Union and the United States are natural leaders and partners.

Swedish envoys also make note of their strong support for human rights. They say that a global commitment to human rights is in Sweden's interests and embodies its aspirations for a fair and honorable world order. Swedes say human rights considerations should be central to all foreign policies, including security, development cooperation, migration, and trade policy. Swedes argue that a coherent human rights policy is relevant to issues such as conflict prevention, migration, asylum, and the fight against terrorism.

Eliasson was passionate about the need to create a culture of prevention and to develop international tools and techniques to prevent humanitarian disasters from occurring. Eliasson spoke often about the political paradox of prevention: however important it may be, there are few political rewards for heading off crises.

"When was the last time you read the headline: the disaster did not occur?" he asked rhetorically. Eliasson is realistic about what has been accomplished so far in the attempt to create this culture of prevention.

"It's hard to identify concrete results, apart from the Macedonia case in 2001. Grim and depressing developments all over the world do not testify to the success of turning prevention into concrete political action," he said.

Swedish diplomats say they strongly support the global fight against terrorism, but argue that it should be done with a careful regard for the rule of law. They have said that Sweden will always be in the vanguard when it comes to fighting terror, but caution that if the fight against terrorism takes priority over human rights, the terrorists will ultimately triumph. Swedish diplomats argue that to defeat international terrorism nations need to combine political commitment, multilateral cooperation, democracy, respect for human rights, and a strategy to combat poverty and avoid failed states.

Eliasson emphasized that Sweden supported the U.S.-led global war on terrorism, but said the prosecution of the war should adhere to the laws of war and the Geneva conventions.

Eliasson at the Pentagon with Sweden's defense minister, Leni Bjorklund

❧ IV ❧

Eliasson made it clear that his single greatest priority as Sweden's ambassador to Washington was to monitor his nation's bilateral relationship with the United States. He worked hard to identify areas where the nations were in accord. For example, Eliasson noted that Sweden shared the United States' commitment to open trade and encouraged other nations to continue trade liberalization policies. Sweden's economy, he emphasized, is fueled by international trade.

Eliasson said that virtually everything that happens politically and economically in the United States could potentially have an impact on his nation. He said American trade and budget deficits had consequences for Sweden's economy as did U.S. policies on homeland security and defense contracts.

❧ V ❧

Like many other nations, Sweden has typically sent its best envoys to Washington. A stream of impressive, senior diplomats has represented Stockholm in the United States. One ambassador, Count Wilhelm

Wachtmeister, served in Washington from 1974 to 1989 and became dean of the diplomatic corps. He was a personal friend of George H. Bush.

Eliasson's immediate predecessor, Rolf Ekeus, was a former chairman of the United Nations Special Commission (UNSCOM) and a respected leader on arms control issues. Ekeus was viewed in Washington more as a global statesman than as a specific advocate for Sweden. A soft-spoken diplomat, his working style appeared very different from that of Eliasson. But Jan Knutsson, a Swedish diplomat who worked for both Ekeus and Eliasson in Washington, said the two were very successful envoys with different styles.

"They have different backgrounds, different personalities but I found they work in very similar ways. What diplomats in Washington have to do is interact with people and build personal relationships with important decision makers—Congress, the White House, the State Department, the think tanks.

"In policy debates you have to be able to understand where the center of gravity is, where decisions are being taken, what particular lines of argument are carrying the most weight at any particular time. You can only do this if you have good relationships at the highest levels. Both Ekeus and Eliasson have a very sharp sense of how systems work—how to push an issue and when to push it and with whom. They immediately recognize an opportunity and know what to do with it."

While Sweden's ambassadors are usually considered highly accomplished, this does not automatically get them the kind of high-level access that is available to the British, Russian, Israeli, or Saudi Arabian ambassadors. Put simply, Sweden's ambassador is not automatically a player in Washington.

CHAPTER 5

Diplomacy in the Capital
of the World

The ambassador with former Secretary of State Colin Powell

꒰ I ꒱

Jan Eliasson brought his vast experience and Sweden's agenda into a Washington that was moving from the final months of the Clinton administration into the new Bush administration. Though the two administrations had vastly different views of the world and the centrality of diplomacy in international relations, the political culture of Washington transcends the peculiar features of each presidential administration.

With the end of the Second World War and especially since the end of the Cold War, Washington has emerged as the political capital of the world. Important diplomacy is conducted in Brussels, Beijing, Paris, London, and Tokyo, but there is little doubt that many of the world's most important decisions are now made in Washington.

Diplomacy is practiced differently in Washington than in any other city in the world. It's a free-wheeling, informal, highly complex scramble to shape the American debate on international affairs and to influence U.S. policies that often have global consequences. Timeless traditions and long-established rules that are scrupulously adhered to in other capitals are often turned on their heads or reformulated in ways that make them unrecognizable.

It's been said that if a diplomat acted in other capitals as he does in Washington, he would be declared persona non grata. But if he doesn't follow these practices in Washington, he will be rebuked for not doing his job. Some experts even contend that a new code of diplomacy is evolving in Washington in which informality, openness, and public advocacy are the driving forces. Diplomats in Washington are expected to be more public, more aggressive, and more willing to plunge into policy debates than in other capitals.

"In most European capitals it is considered rule number one to keep a low profile," said Jón Baldvin Hannibalsson, Iceland's former ambassador to the United States. "In Washington, we're expected to speak, to talk, to peddle our case, and to attract attention."

One of the most distinctive aspects of Washington diplomacy is its sheer size and complexity. More than one hundred eighty nations have embassies there and virtually all are represented by the best envoys they have. Career diplomats, former prime ministers, foreign ministers, and finance ministers are dispatched to Washington. There are not many former used-car salesman or strip-mall developers in Washington. The city has an unusually deep pool of diplomatic talent and political clout.

Additionally, a number of prominent international organizations are based in Washington, such as the World Bank, the International Monetary Fund, the Organization of American States, and the Inter-American Development Bank. Dozens of think tanks, nongovernmental organizations, trade associations, and lobbying groups based in Washington shape policy and are part of the larger diplomatic community. And hundreds of news organizations cover international affairs and influence the city's diplomatic life.

Washington's large, complex diplomatic community is characterized by constantly evolving power configurations. Diplomats from NATO, Group of Seven, European Union, and UN Security Council nations have special access in Washington as do countries with ethnic ties to large or influential domestic groups. Ambassadors from the three *I*s have special visibility in Washington: Ireland, Italy, and Israel.

Washington diplomacy takes on a special complexity given that it is the capital of a large, powerful, and diverse nation in which interest groups can help shape domestic and international policy. A good ambassador in Washington has to be seriously engaged with a wide range of government and nongovernment actors in the United States. A very broad and very deep set of constituencies have to be dealt with directly and constructively for a diplomat to be successful in Washington. This is different from other capitals.

৯৯ II ৯৯

Another feature of Washington diplomacy is the peculiar challenge created by the diffusion of power. In the American government, both the executive and legislative branches play significant roles in formulating international policy. While other nations distribute power between the executive and legislative branches, few do so as broadly and sometimes as confusingly as the American system.

Most diplomats in Washington need to deal at minimum with the White House's National Security Council and the State Department. They also work with the Departments of Agriculture, Commerce, Defense, Energy, Homeland Security, Health and Human Services, Justice, Transportation, Treasury, and the U.S. Trade Representatives Office. In fact, almost every U.S. government agency has its own office of foreign affairs.

The complexity of the executive branch is replicated on Capitol Hill where a bewildering number of committees and subcommittees have important jurisdictions and influence. Congress plays a significant role in crafting international policy. Although the president is the main foreign policy actor, the Constitution delegates more specific foreign policy powers to Congress than the executive. The president is designated as commander in chief and head of the executive branch. Congress is given the power to declare war and to authorize and spend funds. The president can negotiate treaties and nominate foreign policy officials, but the Senate must confirm them. Congress is also empowered to raise and support armies, establish rules on naturalization, regulate foreign commerce, and define and punish offenses on the high seas.

"In Washington, there are one thousand points of decision making," said Walter Cutler, a former American ambassador. "There is a diffusion of decision-making power and because of this ambassadors here are stretched so thin because they have to touch so many bases. They have to cover Washington, both the executive and legislative branches. And they have to go out to the Dulles corridor and Silicon Valley and many, many other places that have an impact on policy and on the economy. Diplomats have to be aware of the views and influence of dozens of interest groups that have a real impact. To be effective, an ambassador can't just sit in his office and make formal calls on other diplomats. That doesn't work in this city."

Diplomats say that to be successful in Washington they have to be willing to discuss and debate policy issues with key government actors and private interest groups.

"The U.S. is a country of advocacy. To be successful here, you have to engage with all the people, not just with the government. In no other place that I'm aware of does domestic politics meet with foreign policy at such an intense level," said Nabil Fahmy, Egypt's ambassador to the United States.

The ambassador with Secretary of State Condoleezza Rice and White House Chief of Staff Andrew Card

"One learns in Washington not to be offended easily. Americans like you to say what you really think. The level of debate is very candid, very frank. In a more formal system an ambassador might have to make arguments differently, less directly and less frankly. But here candor and directness are expected and appreciated."

Almost all diplomats note the informality of Washington diplomacy. "In European capitals, things are much more formal. Here it is quite open. People often come up to you and they don't even ask where you are from. They ask: 'What do you have to say? What are your arguments?' There is more equality of opportunity here than in more formal systems," Hannibalsson said.

ໆ III ໆ

In many diplomatic centers, ambassadors form a close-knit community that meets often, socializes frequently, and presents a unified front to the host government. In Washington, ambassadors from the more than one hundred eighty countries usually have little to do with each other, except with ambassadors who are from the same region.

"Everybody here is working on their own. There are no teams. Everybody is so busy and they are working by themselves. We don't see much of our colleagues except at receptions," said George Saliba, Malta's former ambassador to Washington.

There is a clear competitive aspect to Washington diplomacy; each ambassador and embassy is trying to win the notice and respect of the administration, Congress, and the press. The scramble to get noticed, listened to, and taken seriously is fierce.

Jan Eliasson said that while he enjoyed his fellow ambassadors in Washington, he spent limited time with them. He did meet frequently with ambassadors from the European Union and specifically from northern Europe, but had much less contact with other envoys.

"This is a bilateral city," he said, adding that his main focus was developing good relations with the administration and Congress as well as others who shape the political debate in Washington.

ໆ IV ໆ

Allan Gotlieb, a former Canadian ambassador to Washington, has written an illuminating memoir about his years in Washington, *I'll Be with You in a Minute, Mr. Ambassador: The Education of a Canadian Diplomat in Washington,* in which he argues that diplomats need to unlearn much of what they know about diplomacy. Gotlieb says he was trained, like all diplomats, to deal with power that is readily identifiable, defined, and focused. He was trained to conduct diplomacy discreetly behind closed doors, where visibility and the limelight are to be avoided and where confidentiality is the norm. But he argues that traditional diplomacy in Washington is a recipe for ineffectiveness or even irrelevance. He says the two traditional injunctions about diplomacy are particularly irrelevant in Washington: ambassadors should work primarily with the foreign ministry and they shouldn't intervene in the domestic affairs of the host country.

An ambassador in Washington, Gotlieb says, must work with a wide range of actors "that are constantly shifting, aligning and realigning in ways that can affect or damage the interests of the country he represents." Additionally, ambassadors need to develop specific strategies on each issue they address and be willing to make their cases publicly and aggressively.

Like many other diplomats who have worked in Washington, Gotlieb is a strong believer in the importance of social life as the lifeblood of diplomacy. He argues that the best and often the only way to gain access to important political, business, media, and cultural actors in Washington is through the social route.

"To be the hottest embassy in Washington was my chief diplomatic asset in a town where most diplomats are permanently marginalized," he writes.

Hope Ridings Miller, an expert on Washington diplomacy, writes in her book *Embassy Row* that social events are one of the best ways for diplomats to meet with American leaders. She said that the capital's social structure enables ambassadors to get around, get acquainted, and get attention where it counts. And if ambassadors entertain often and graciously enough, they can make important contacts in short order.

Miller quotes Australia's Sir Howard Beale describing, more than forty years ago, the centrality of social life in Washington diplomacy:

> Society is an important part of the diplomatic game. Success depends on building confidence for one's country on a person-to-person basis. The logical way to begin—the only graceful way, in fact, is through social contact. We envoys can't haunt the halls of Congress, the State Department and the White House to get acquainted with the people we need to know. We have to entertain and be entertained, in order to meet them. The real work, the hard work, comes after that. A diplomat's career is like an iceberg. The glittering part shows; the other is below the surface.

ৡ V ৡ

When John and Abigail Adams traveled from Philadelphia to Washington in 1800 to move into the executive mansion, seven foreign countries had opened relations with the United States, but only four were represented by ministers, the top diplomats of that time: Great Britain, France, the Netherlands, and Spain. At that time, the entire foreign corps was less than twenty people. And only twelve diplomats attended the first social affair, the 1801 New Year's reception in the president's house.

Over the next two centuries the diplomatic corps in Washington grew steadily. From only a handful of diplomatic establishments in 1801, Washington's diplomatic community grew to more than 100 missions by the end of the Eisenhower administration, 118 missions by 1967, and now is up to 185 embassies.

In 1900, most of the diplomatic missions were located on 16th Street—a section that came to be known as Embassy Row. But what was called Embassy Row expanded in the 1930s when the British opened a glittering diplomatic establishment on upper Massachusetts Avenue. Other embassies followed and it took over as the locus of Washington diplomacy.

With the demand for embassy real estate growing, Congress passed legislation in 1968 to create a diplomatic enclave of thirty-four acres in northwest Washington. The State Department worked with city and federal officials to establish the International Chancery Center. It offers building sites where fifteen countries have constructed office buildings since the 1980s.

Of the 185 embassies in Washington, the size of national delegations ranges from two or three to hundreds. While some nations may own or rent a modest townhouse for their chancery and a small residence for their ambassador, other nations own palatial buildings and office buildings. The British, for example, own more than seventy buildings in Washington.

In recent years, more than a dozen countries have built or are in the midst of building large, glittering embassies. The goal of the embassies is to reach the broadest possible audience in hopes of being heard above the din of other countries competing for attention in Washington.

Diplomats say it has become increasingly difficult to attract leaders from Congress and the administration to dinners and receptions. Even with their gleaming edifices, the embassies must come up with ever more exciting events to attract attention. Ambassadors say it's important to work in the humanitarian, cultural, and social spheres.

৯৯ VI ৯৯

The skills required to be a successful diplomat are broadly similar in all capitals, but Washington poses specific challenges. These arise from the free-wheeling nature of the political system in the United States and from the country's status as the world's political capital. Analysts agree that in assessing ambassadorial power in Washington a crucial factor is the country the envoy represents and its relationship with the United States. The most technically skilled ambassador in the world representing a pariah country will not be successful in Washington. Other factors include the diplomatic tradition and support system the ambassador has and the specific issues that are important in Washington during the time of service.

But less tangible factors are also important, including diplomatic skill, political savvy, and personal charm. Henry Catto, a former American ambassador to the United Kingdom and former chief of protocol, said personal skills are difficult to overstate. "A gregarious and charming personality is very important for an ambassador—in Washington and elsewhere. A grumpy ambassador is not going to have much clout," he said.

Catto added that having a solid understanding of how decisions are made in Washington is crucial. "Very few ambassadors really understand what is going on in Washington and how decisions are made," he said.

Analysts agree that there are different types of ambassadors in Washington. First, there are those who represent nations with extensive and complicated bilateral relationships with the United States such as Canada, Mexico, Egypt, Pakistan, and, increasingly, China. These ambassadors spend most of their time trying to solve specific problems and often run large embassies.

Canada's Washington embassy has more than two hundred fifty people who deal with a bewildering array of issues that range from border security to mad cow disease to softwood lumber. Other ambassadors represent nations that have few bilateral issues with the United States and are here largely to monitor events and make sure no serious problems arise. Some diplomats lobby Congress and the administration to secure foreign assistance or military aid. Others are here to monitor their bilateral relationship but also to help influence the debate in Washington.

The two most celebrated ambassadors of the past half century are Anatoly Dobrynin, who was the Soviet ambassador from 1962 to 1986, and Prince Bandar of Saudi Arabia, who was ambassador from 1983 to 2005. Both represented countries that were of considerable political and strategic importance to the United States. But both had special qualities.

Dobrynin served as a crucial conduit of information between the leaders of the two superpowers during the hard days of the Cold War. He played a critical role in defusing the Cuban Missile Crisis by holding private talks with Robert Kennedy, a key advisor to his brother during the crisis.

Bandar, Saudi Arabia's ambassador, represented a nation of immense strategic and political importance to the United States. Additionally, Bandar had high-level access, great personal skills, and a reputation for getting things done. Unlike almost every other ambassador in Washington, he was able to meet with the president whenever he felt he needed to.

Charles W. Freeman, Jr., a former American ambassador to Saudi Arabia who has also written extensively on diplomacy, said Bandar was probably the most influential ambassador in Washington during the last quarter of the twentieth century.

"He had incredible access. He had great personal skills. He had a reputation for getting things done. He could deliver. He was sort of a man's man. Presidents trusted him," Freeman says.

Senate Foreign Relations Committee Chairman, Richard Lugar, said ambassadors should not necessarily seek to achieve Bandar's level of visibility and prominence.

"Bandar was certainly very visible. But you can be very effective as an ambassador without enormous visibility. Pursuing your objectives quietly and competently and diligently can be very effective," he said.

Lugar believes that effective ambassadors in Washington tend to have certain qualities. First, they almost always have a strong familiarity with the United Sates, an understanding that is often rooted in either time spent here as a student or an earlier diplomatic posting.

Lugar said successful ambassadors usually come from countries that have a positive, non-contentious diplomatic relationship with the United States. "At a minimum, the relationship should not be a bad one," he said.

Good Washington ambassadors very often have engaging personalities that are able to deal with all segments of Washington's diplomatic community in very different contexts. They need to know when to be serious and when to be relaxed.

Successful ambassadors are generally able to find interesting ways and programs to bring Washington leaders to their embassies. They take advantage of visits from cultural and political leaders from home to plan engaging events. "It's helpful if they can make a visit to their embassy memorable and enjoyable," he said.

Finally, successful ambassadors almost always have a solid support staff behind them that allows them to be well briefed and able to be responsive and ideally, proactive.

Casimir Yost, an expert on diplomacy at the Institute for the Study of Diplomacy at Georgetown University, said that ambassadors in Washington should begin their work by accepting one obvious but often painful truth: Life in Washington is not fair.

"In Washington some ambassadors are more equal than others. That's just how it works. Some ambassadors have more natural prominence than others. For example, ambassadors from Israel, the UK, France, and Germany tend to be more visible than others. But all ambassadors have to work with a much broader swathe of society than they do in other capitals," Yost said.

They need to make high-level contacts with Congress, the White House, and the diplomatic community in Washington. They also need to build a social network, connect with the press, manage an embassy, reach out to business leaders, cultivate expatriate communities, meet political and business leaders outside of Washington, and explain their countries' views to American leaders and describe the views of the American leadership back home.

Singapore's ambassador to the United States, Chan Heng Chee, said that ambassadors in Washington must be constantly looking for ways to advance their countries' relationship with the U.S

"People don't think of diplomacy this way, but ambassadors really are political entrepreneurs. You have to be entrepreneurial. You have to see opportunities to enhance your representation. Every ambassador must play to his or her strength to advance their bilateral relationship with the United States," she said.

CHAPTER 6

Connecting Washington
and Stockholm

Eliasson bantering with Senator George Allen and M. Teel Bivins, at his confirmation hearing to be the U.S. ambassador to Sweden.

ॐ **I** ॐ

During receptions at his residence, Jan Eliasson would typically assemble his guests by ringing a bell and then, when the people were gathered around

53

him, offer a few remarks in the form of a toast. While his comments varied depending on the theme of the specific reception and the guests invited, Eliasson often found a way to emphasize one overriding message.

There was a critical need, he said, for both Swedes and other Europeans to take a "mental Atlantic journey" to the United States and for Americans to make a similar journey to Europe. What the ambassador was referring to was the importance of Swedes and Europeans trying to put themselves into the minds of Americans and see the world from their perspective. And alternately, Americans should try to see the world from the perspective of the European, even from a small nation such as Sweden.

Eliasson said that Swedes and other Europeans should understand that the United States, as the world's dominant power, can decide how it wants to operate on the world stage. "Whether we like it or not, a superpower has choices; it act can multilaterally, it can act unilaterally, or it can lead a coalition of the willing," he said. Put differently, American leaders could decide if they wanted to go alone, work with the rest of the world, or work with a few, select partners.

His fellow countrymen and other Europeans, Eliasson said, should recognize that the United States was deeply changed by the terrorist attacks of September 11, 2001. Americans felt more threatened than they had for most of their history and were willing to support extraordinary measures that they believed would advance their security.

"The doctrine of military preemption cannot be understood without the mental journey across the Atlantic to the 9/11 events," he said. But in turn, the ambassador said, the United States should understand that Swedes and other Europeans have their own view of the world that has been shaped by their historic experiences. These experiences, he said, have persuaded them that multinational cooperation and respect for international law and norms are the best way to maintain peace and ensure safety and prosperity.

"In Europe for one thousand years we tried to solve our problems by military means," he said. After the Second World War, European leaders sought a different way and responded by creating the European Union and working with global institutions such as the United Nations.

In no small way, Eliasson's years as ambassador to Washington had as their central feature his attempt to serve as a travel guide on this mental transatlantic journey. More specifically, Eliasson served as an interpreter between the people and government of Sweden and the people and government of the United States. He tried to explain Sweden to America and America to Sweden. And once the two countries were speaking the same language, Eliasson tried to make deep and important connections—connections that would transcend specific issues or ambassadors.

As a native of Sweden, but as a person who had spent more than a decade in the United States during his career, Eliasson understood that Washington and Stockholm are very different places and that the leaders in these capitals often see the world quite differently.

❧ II ❧

If Washington is the bustling capital of the twenty-first century built on a muggy swamp, Stockholm is a quiet, cool, serene, almost medieval city that sprawls over fourteen islands that separate the Baltic Sea from Lake Malaren. Founded more than seven hundred fifty years ago, Stockholm was an important port in the German-dominated Hanseatic League that controlled the Baltic Sea region for centuries. Stockholm later became the center of a Swedish empire that ruled northern Europe for much of the seventeenth century.

Stockholm is a beautiful, quaint European capital, which is sometimes called "the Venice of the North." Home to more than a million people, nearly one hundred embassies, and a number of multinational firms, it is hardly a backwater. But it's not the diplomatic center of the world. And it doesn't aspire to be. In fact, Sweden's historical experience with hegemony was a distasteful one. As a great power between 1611 and 1721, it was at war most of the time. Swedes long ago lost their appetite for conquest and bloodshed.

An important part of Eliasson's job in Washington was explaining Sweden's view of the world and foreign policy agenda to American leaders and the larger public. Sweden, in Eliasson's narrative, is a medium-sized nation that is an active member of the increasingly consequential European Union. It is also a natural leader of the Nordic-Baltic community that is a region of good news in a troubled world.

Eliasson also argued that Sweden is a serious and engaged nation with global views, aspirations, and commitments. It has been willing to offer its treasure to support development and send its young peacekeepers to bring stability to troubled places. The ambassador emphasized that Sweden was participating in important reconstruction missions in Afghanistan and the Balkans and in humanitarian work in Sudan. He also said that Sweden had informed views and interesting perspectives on the greater Middle East, Palestine and Israel, and Russia. The ambassador noted that geography and history have given Swedes a nuanced and sophisticated understanding of Russia.

His nation, he also argued, had serious views on promoting human rights, stemming the proliferation of weapons of mass destruction, confronting global warming, preserving the environment, and defeating terrorism.

Eliasson presented Sweden's view of the world to Washington's diplomatic community in subtle ways. "In diplomacy it's important to have a light touch. When you're always delivering a heavy message people get tired of you," he says.

Connecting with the administration was his chief concern, and like many ambassadors, his dealings were primarily with the State Department and the National Security Council, but included the Departments of Agriculture, Commerce, Defense, Justice, Health and Human Services, and Treasury, as well as the U.S. trade representative's office.

Within the State Department, he worked most closely with the European bureau, which had specialists dealing with Nordic and Swedish issues. He had a pleasant, cordial relationship the three secretaries of state he worked with: Madeleine Albright, Colin Powell, and Condoleezza Rice and their deputies, especially the various assistant secretaries for European affairs.

At the NSC, he dealt with Rice when she was the NSC chief and her successor, Stephen Hadley, as well as with Elliott Abrams and Damon Wilson. He attended nearly weekly meetings at State and the NSC and maintained contacts with key officials in frequent phone calls.

Eliasson also developed important relations on Capitol Hill, focusing on the House International Affairs and Senate Foreign Relations committees, especially each panel's European subcommittee. Sweden does not typically have many issues before Congress, but Eliasson tried to stay connected to Capitol Hill, though he acknowledged his approach to congressional outreach was more intuitive than systematic.

In addition to taking Sweden's message to the legislative and executive branches, Eliasson actively worked with the think tank community and the press. Eliasson says that he tried hard to add a Swedish and European perspective to policy debates. He aspired to be a "reasonable European voice."

Eliasson argues that to get a seat at the policy-making table in Washington you have to have something substantive to say. "The simple fact is you have to be interesting. I have to take a strong European position or talk about issues that I have an expertise in: Iran and Iraq, mediation, the UN and transatlantic relations.

"In Washington, if you are a Russian or British ambassador you are automatically taken seriously. But if you are a Swedish ambassador you have to be well briefed and well prepared. You have to have something interesting to contribute. That's why I'm reading so much. That's why I'm well prepared when I go to meetings. And if I can be a pretty good ambassador in the EU context, it adds to their interest in me."

During his time in Washington, Eliasson tried to focus on common values and shared goals with the United States, but sometimes he had to express Sweden's disagreement with the United States. "Diplomacy is not always about agreeing. It's being able to express disagreements in a clear and constructive way," he said.

Eliasson conveyed to the Bush administration Sweden's strong views about Iraq, especially in the months leading up to the start of the war in early 2003. Specifically, he argued that while the Swedish government had no love for Saddam Hussein, it believed that the only basis for a U.S.-led invasion, absent an attack by Iraq, was if it was supported by the UN Security Council. In the run-up to the war, Eliasson made it clear that Swedish leaders would not be silent on the administration's decision to act without what it regarded as UN approval.

"I think the American administration expected us to have this position. I didn't hide our views. I said I represented the country of Dag Hammarskjöld and told them that the foreign minister and the prime minister would say things they would not like. I said it exactly that way," he recalled.

Eliasson also said that he did not discourage Swedish leaders from expressing their opposition to the war. "I told Stockholm we should say what we believe. In any mature relationship, you have to expect there will be different points of view. You have a deeper friendship if you have discussions on issues where you part company," he said.

Eliasson also spent long hours in talks with the administration on the detention of a Swedish prisoner at Guantanamo Bay. Swedish government officials, including the prime minister and the foreign minister, argued publicly that their prisoner should either be charged with a crime or set free. In talks with State Department officials, Eliasson expressed this view strongly. He was also careful to explain how politically important and even explosive this issue had become in Swedish domestic politics.

"Jan was very good at explaining to all of us how important this issue was back home. He gave us a Swedish domestic perspective that put the issue in a broader context," said Beth Jones, a former assistant secretary of state for European affairs.

In the end, Eliasson working with various levels of State Department officials and senior Defense Department officials got the matter resolved. "This was a sort of negotiation, In fact, it was a classic case of negotiation. We could have blown it. It was a choreographed negotiation," he said.

Heather Conley, a senior State Department official who dealt with Eliasson on the issue, said the ambassador was constructive and helpful in resolving the matter—but said the prisoner was released only when Sweden agreed to a series of conditions.

ഇ III ഇ

On a typical day, Eliasson woke up at 7 or 7:30 a.m.—"sort of late by Washington standards" he says a little sheepishly. He read the morning newspapers "very carefully in a comfortable chair"—reviewing stories about U.S. domestic politics and foreign policy. He listened to National Public Radio as he got dressed.

The ambassador had breakfast that was prepared by the embassy's chef at 8:30 a.m., placing several calls to Sweden during his meal to get a feel for what Sweden's foreign policy and political leaders were doing and thinking about.

He left his home at about 9. As his Volvo limousine eased down Nebraska and Massachusetts avenues toward downtown Washington he scanned articles from Swedish newspapers that were faxed to him by his assistant, Monica Lundkvist.

Eliasson usually arrived at the Swedish embassy in downtown Washington at 15th and M at about 9:30 a.m. Twice a week he presided over a meeting of embassy staff, which was referred to as "morning prayer." The meeting was designed to give him an overview of what was going on at the embassy.

Since Stockholm is six hours ahead of Washington, Eliasson took care of any business he needed to do with people at home before noon. "I do the Swedish agenda in the morning," he says.

He often attended late-morning or noontime sessions at Washington's various think tanks, especially the Brookings Institution, the Woodrow Wilson Center, the U.S. Institute of Peace, which is only several blocks from the Swedish embassy, and the Center for Strategic and International Studies (CSIS), which has an extensive European program. Early in his tenure, he decided to invest time and energy in getting plugged into the think tank community.

Richard Solomon, president of the Institute of Peace, and Simon Serfaty, head of the CSIS's European program, both said that Eliasson was one of the few ambassadors who regularly attended programs, even when he was not a speaker or on a panel.

Think tanks, Eliasson argues, play a crucial role in formulating policy alternatives. He believed that attending seminars and meetings gave him a chance to present Sweden's views on issues and allowed him to offer ideas that move up the Washington policy food chain. It also gave him a context in which to meet policy leaders in the United States and get a sense of what Washington's foreign policy community was thinking about and expecting to happen in the future.

The ambassador liked to use his residence to host small working lunches of about a dozen people to discuss a specific issue or project that Sweden is particularly interested in. These sessions, which had the feel and format of high-level graduate school seminars, ran from 12:30 p.m. to 2 p.m. He used the time in his limousine before and after these meetings to catch up on reading, banter with his engaging and politically savvy driver, Zigurs "Zig" Liepins, return phone calls, and call his staff about pending matters. "We all pray he doesn't get stuck in traffic," a Swedish diplomat told me. "Those are the times the phone calls come pouring in."

The ambassador had an open-door policy and his staff was encouraged to drop by to discuss an issue, review a cable, or bring visitors by for a brief chat. The ambassador was an amiable but demanding boss with a penchant for micromanagment that he tried—sometimes—to restrain. But he was also keenly aware of morale at his embassy.

He usually left the office at 6 p.m., but this was just the start of his second shift. He often stopped at receptions on his way home. Like many busy cabinet secretaries, diplomats, and lawmakers, Eliasson perfected the art of the fifteen-minute drop-in.

"It's important to show very clearly that you are there and then you can sneak out," he says.

When he returned home, he showered, watched the BBC evening news and then often went out for a formal dinner or event. He enjoyed the city's party scene and found those gatherings a good way to have fun, expand his network, and learn about what is really going on.

Eliasson said his social life changed fundamentally in February 2004 when his wife returned to Stockholm to serve as the deputy minister of education.

"We used to go to formal dinners quite often. But I did this far less often after Kerstin left. Washington is a couples' town. I just didn't feel comfortable going to a lot of dinners without her," he said.

He set aside a few hours every evening, usually between 10 p.m. and midnight, to work through piles of documents that gathered in the corner of his library. He sat in a comfortable red chair, chewing on a cigar, sipping a glass of wine, and listening to classical music as he worked away. He read cables, articles from foreign policy magazines, and books on international affairs. When the heavy lifting was done, Eliasson plunged into Swedish newspapers, catching up on politics, sports, business, and gossip from home.

"I'm not here forever. I want to know what's going on back home. You have to have a sense of your own country," he says.

He had notepads sprinkled around his house where he scrawled notes when ideas came to him. He gathered these notes in the morning and often dumped them on Lundkvist's desk. She would organize the ideas and figure out what kind of responses were required.

ॐ **IV** ॐ

In the key interactions between the Swedish and American governments, Eliasson tried to keep his embassy deeply engaged and, if possible, in the lead role.

"We have the best overview of the relationship, the best analysis of how to reach people in power. We have the best analysis of the realities on the ground. We see the realities here," Eliasson said.

"If you have a good ambassador you should give them more responsibility and power. We should play a role in preparing policy. My dispatches say, 'I suggest we do this,'" he added.

While trying to keep Sweden's views part of the American debate and solving any problems in the bilateral relationship, Eliasson exerted considerable energy in explaining America to the government and people of Sweden. Swedes, even those senior in the government, are aware of what is going on in the United States but often don't understand why, how the decisions were made, and, crucially, what will happen in the future.

"The United States is the most important country in the world. This is Sweden's most important bilateral relationship. My reports back home get a high readership," Eliasson said.

Informal and well known in Sweden's diplomatic establishment, Eliasson would tap into his vast network in Stockholm to get a sense of what the government was interested in and concerned about. Depending on the topic and urgency, he would call the prime minister's chief of staff, the foreign minister, the deputy foreign minister, the chief of the Foreign Ministry's Americas unit, or others in the Foreign Ministry to gauge interests and moods.

Eliasson also made it a point to draft every six weeks a seven- or eight-page cable about political developments in the United States. He tried to use this as a vehicle to outline big themes. His cables were typically sent to the foreign minister and prime minister's office as well as the Americas Department in the Foreign Ministry. A senior Swedish diplomat based in Stockholm said Eliasson was constantly on the alert for Swedish leaders expressing disagreements in personal terms rather than in policy statements.

"We had Jan on the phone constantly telling us not to be too tough in our statements. But on the other hand, I have no doubt he's conveying our message to the State Department in a clear and firm manner," the diplomat said.

The American embassy in Stockholm carefully monitored Swedish politics and the press and informed Washington of any comments they felt were inflammatory or required an American response or a Swedish one. Swedish diplomats say the Americans were quick to find offense in comments made by junior lawmakers. Conley, the former State department official, says the United States was mostly concerned when senior members of the Swedish government blasted the United States.

"A number of times I had to call the ambassador and say this comment from Stockholm is very unhelpful. He would look into it, place it in its broader context, and sometimes get it clarified. He understood our concerns," Conley said.

Eliasson kept Stockholm apprised of developments in the United States by organizing visits from senior government officials and parliamentarians to Washington. He also encouraged Americans to come to Stockholm. Eliasson would typically brief Swedish visitors about his assessment of the American-Swedish relationship before they had their meetings with counterparts in the U.S. government and in the think tank and business communities.

The ambassador also traveled frequently to Stockholm for meetings at the foreign ministry. He was careful to make it a point to meet with parliamentarians interested in foreign affairs and developments in the United States. Göran Lennmarker, chairman of the Swedish parliament's Constitution Committee, said Eliasson frequently briefed him when he returned to Sweden and made a point to meet with Lennmarker when he was in Washington.

"Every time I was in Washington and he knew it he made time to see me—to squeeze in a few minutes for coffee or a ride to the airport or to have lunch at his residence," he said.

The ambassador also was a frequent guest on Swedish television, explaining what was going on in the United States. Urben Ahlin, the chairman of the Foreign Relations Committee, said Eliasson is adept at explaining foreign policy on television and in public events.

"He's a natural talent on TV. He uses colorful language. He paints pictures with his words. Every good leader does that. Eliasson has that ability.

*Eliasson talking to Urben Ahlin, the chairman of the Swedish parliament's foreign
affairs committee*

He brings traditional Swedish values even as he explains new challenges. He
makes people feel comfortable," he said.

Eliasson was also willing to speak more difficult truths to Stockholm, but
his warnings were not always heeded. At one point, the Swedish government
was pushing the candidacy of a former development minister for a senior UN
post for the reconstruction of Kosovo. This person had written sharply critical comments about the United States–a fact that Eliasson thought could be
a problem. Eliasson suggested that he quietly work with the administration
to see if he could build support for the candidate. But the Swedish government went forward with the nomination and tried to skirt potential
American objections by describing the nomination as a European choice.
State Department officials objected and worked with Eliasson to have the
name withdrawn.

"I said to Stockholm, let me work with the Americans and see if this candidacy will fly. I told them, with the Americans you don't play games. I think
I could have made the case. But they tried a different approach. It didn't work."

Eliasson preferred going beyond explaining the views of Washington to Stockholm and of Stockholm to Washington. He relished connecting leaders and peoples and introducing the personal element into diplomacy.

"My main task is to be a link to the American administration and the Congress and the political life in Washington. This is the superpower of the world. Ambassadors should devote their time to building bridges in this country," he said.

And he believed that Sweden received an important seat at the table in Washington. "I notice we are invited to meetings, along with the British, French, and Germans. I think we have put ourselves on the map. I'm extremely proud of that. For me, it's crucial that our visibility be maintained. We should be seen as an actor in this city. I'm here on the taxpayer's money to represent Sweden. This is not a personal chair."

CHAPTER 7

The Networker

Eliasson with Powell and Sweden's foreign minister, Laila Freivalds

❧ I ❧

In the spring of 2005, Jan Eliasson was on the phone with Sweden's international development minister, Carin Jamtin. In the course of the conversation, Jamtin said she and some of her EU counterparts had concerns about the candidacy of Paul Wolfowitz to become the president of the World Bank. She told the ambassador that she had a number of questions she would like to ask Wolfowitz, such as his views on African development, UN reform, and poverty reduction.

"Then why don't you give him a call," Eliasson said.

When Jamtin wondered how easily it would be to get through to Wolfowitz, Eliasson said that he could arrange it. He immediately called the Pentagon and was transferred to Wolfowitz. They bantered for a moment and then the ambassador got to the point.

"I was very direct with him," Eliasson recalled, noting that Wolfowitz's nomination to become World Bank president was greeted with concern and even incredulity by some European officials, especially from development ministers. Eliasson suggested that Wolfowitz speak to Jamtin, Sweden's development minister, who was active among development ministers in the European Union.

"I said you have a problem with Europe. I told him point blank: Paul, it will be good for you to have that conversation," Eliasson said. Within an hour, Jamtin and Wolfowitz were on the phone talking about his vision of the World Bank and his views on a host of specific issues. And Jamtin later arranged a meeting in Brussels where Wolfowitz met with key EU development ministers who asked him questions and then dropped any talk of trying to derail his bid to the World Bank presidency.

The entire episode was a win for all parties. Wolfowitz secured the World Bank presidency and Jamtin got her questions answered and received gratitude from her EU colleagues for setting up the important meeting. Eliasson received thanks from Wolfowitz, the gratitude of the Swedish government, and he bolstered his reputation in Stockholm as an ambassador with high-level connections that could be used to get things done.

The fact is that very few ambassadors in Washington could have gotten Wolfowitz on the phone within an hour. But Eliasson knew him from the extensive dealings they had on negotiating the release of the Swedish prisoner at Guantanamo. But even those conversations were made possible by social encounters the two men had. Both were guests of *Newsweek* at the 2004 White House correspondents dinner and sat at the same table. The *Newsweek* table is distinctly A-list and Wolfowitz no doubt took note that Eliasson was the guest of Lally Weymouth, an influential columnist for *Newsweek* and the daughter of Katharine Graham.

"It was a pretty high-level table," Eliasson said with a smile. In Washington, social contacts are an integral part of conducting business.

৯৯ II ৯৯

As Eliasson prepared to come to Washington in late summer of 2000, he reflected on the many components of an ambassador's job. But he was very clear about his fundamental goal: to develop high-level contacts in the administration, Congress, and the other parts of Washington's political and international affairs community. In the course of his time in Washington, Eliasson built a network that most embassies in Washington would have died for. It included administration officials, lawmakers, think tank leaders, socialites, journalists, business executives, cultural leaders, and most of the Supreme Court.

He developed an impressive network of luminaries—some would call it a salon—that kept him plugged into a steady stream of information. This allowed him to understand what was going on in the United States and to articulate Sweden's message to an important audience. It was unusual to attend a dinner or reception at the Swedish embassy and not see a Supreme Court justice, a senior American diplomat, or a significant congressional staffer. Eliasson's network was built conversation by conversation, business card by business card, reception by reception. It was woven by a naturally engaging and socially skilled man.

"I don't have any secrets. Creating a network is irrational. Or maybe instinctive is a better word," he said.

But Eliasson's network was created by a diplomat with a clear purpose: to cultivate contacts representing all aspects of Washington life who could provide information, offer perspectives, and be activated at the appropriate time.

Eliasson, like all ambassadors, inherited his predecessor's network, which was based both on his personal contacts and long-standing friends of the embassy. "The network that was in place when I arrived was Rolf Ekeus's network. He was Mr. Iraq and Mr. UNSCOM. His contacts were in the Iraq realm. They were high-level contacts," he said. "But you can't automatically take over your predecessor's network. You have to create your own," he added.

Creating a Washington network requires the purposeful pursuit of relationships, fortuitous encounters, good luck, and on occasion, sheer audacity. For an ambassador, it means hitting the party circuit, meeting people, exchanging cards, and then following up with phone calls, notes, E-mails, and invitations to embassy events. While some disparage the social dimension of the diplomatic life, Eliasson said it is essential.

"When you go to a reception you are working. It can be fun, but you are working. You can't be a gray mouse sitting in a corner gathering dust and writing brilliant reports based on the *Washington Post* or *New York Times* and think you are a good ambassador," he said.

"Washington requires a 9 a.m. to 11 p.m. day. The social life is work. I'm always performing, sending messages, exchanging cards, writing notes, arranging meetings. It's a pretty tough job. Hard work, hard work," he said, mimicking President Bush.

Eliasson believed that an important part of his job was to make the Swedish embassy a fun and interesting place to visit. This included a relaxed atmosphere with an interesting and diverse mix of people.

"If the rumor spreads that your embassy is a place where people have fun and stimulating conversations, it's an advantage. And you should have good food," he said.

He tried to spread his contacts into new fields and he used his wife's work as the embassy's science counselor to embrace her network in science and research.

"Kerstin developed an impressive range of contacts in the scientific and research community in the United States. This helped us expand our network into a new area. It was very important."

৯ III ৯

While Eliasson's network appeared to be the natural consequence of the work of an extroverted and engaging man, a lot of work and planning was behind it. The nerve center for the Swedish network was a small, quiet, orderly office on the ninth floor of the embassy's chancery, a floor below Eliasson's office. Gunilla Stone, the ambassador's social secretary, is an elegant, soft-spoken, gracious woman. She keeps a record of embassy parties and receptions in colored binders. She plans future events in a calm, methodical way.

The Swedish embassy hosts about four thousand visitors a year. By contrast, the British embassy hosts about one thousand guests a week. But almost everyone involved in social diplomacy will tell you that the number of guests is less important than who the guests are.

The Swedish embassy has a master list of eight hundred guests who are invited to events based on who is being honored and what the occasion is. But the list is an organic one—names are added and subtracted as people enter and leave jobs.

"We've never had a list as large as this before, but a lot of it is Jan's personality. He comes back from something, gives me some cards, and asks me to put them on the list," Stone said.

The embassy has a $3.4 million annual budget and a $140,000 entertainment budget. The ambassador gets about $90,000 and use of the residence and a limousine. Stone worked closely with Eliasson's personal assistant, Monica Lundkvist, a warm, high-energy, perpetually friendly woman. Stone and Lundkvist tried to develop a system with weekly meetings with the ambassador to plan events, but gave up trying to set aside formal meetings with Eliasson.

"You never get to sit down with him very long because the telephone rings all the time," Stone says.

Stone and Lundkvist developed a more informal system that worked for Eliasson. Parties or receptions are typically scheduled around the visit to Washington of a government minister, or group of parliamentarians, or a Swedish cultural group. A date for an event is set without worrying about what other parties are occurring that night.

"You can never have a night in Washington when nothing is going on. If you tried to do that you'd never schedule anything," Stone said. Typically, Stone would draw up a preliminary guest list and place it in the ambassador's in-box. Eliasson would mark it up, adding names and subtracting others.

"We've developed a very good system. It works very well," Stone said.

During much of Eliasson's time in Washington, the embassy would host on average one major reception a week as well as several working lunches. On occasion, Eliasson hosted a larger group of up to one hundred fifty for cocktails and hors d'oeuvres or a sit-down dinner in his dinning room for about forty. But his preferred event was a buffet for about seventy-five people, typically running from 6:30 p.m. to 8:30 p.m. or 7 p.m. to 9 p.m.

After drinks and a toast, guests would be escorted into the dining room and told to help themselves to a wonderful selection of Swedish food. Guests would then go off in small groups to eat and mingle.

"People want to have more freedom, to cut it short, to go to another table with their glass of wine," the ambassador said.

Eliasson's predecessor, Ekeus, preferred small dinners and few receptions. Stone said Eliasson tried to avoid large parties. "Jan doesn't want massive parties. It's hard to keep track of what's going on," she said.

Eliasson liked to use his residence for lunch meetings, which would usually focus on a specific topic such as land mines or UN reform. He often invited another ambassador to participate and sometimes administration officials.

At his first lunch in 2001, Condoleezza Rice, then head of the NSC, was invited as were the ambassadors from the other nations of the European Union.

Sweden at that time held the rotating presidency of the European Union and the lunch was a chance to hear from administration. It became more newsworthy than Eliasson's other lunches.

"That's when she proclaimed the Kyoto Protocol was 'dead on arrival.' When she said it almost all the ambassadors turned over their menus and began to write notes. I think about fifteen cables were sent out after that lunch," he recalls. "It came out two days later in the *Financial Times*," he adds.

The ambassador and the author

❧ IV ❧

When hosting a party, Jan Eliasson is confident, polished, prepared, and effective. While there is natural skill involved, Eliasson said that hosting a successful reception is work. It requires that you think about what kind of people you want to invite, consider how they might interact, and decide what you want to accomplish.

After working carefully with Stone and Lundkvist to prepare the most appropriate guest list, Eliasson typically would spend fifteen minutes before a reception going over the list, reminding himself what guests would be in attendance, what they do, and how they are connected to him and the embassy.

"It's important to combine different people who fit well together. Putting together a good party list takes more time than you think. And I'm very careful about the toasts I prepare. I think about it and prepare, even if it doesn't look prepared," he said

A few minutes before the reception was set to start, he would go down to the first floor and greet guests as they arrived, almost always by name. If there was one guest of honor he would introduce this person to the other guests. Once everyone arrived, he would circulate around the room, making introductions, and telling guests about each other.

"People are flattered when you know something about them," he said.

About forty-five minutes into the reception, Eliasson would stand on a step overlooking the main reception room and give a brief toast, invariably beginning with "Dear Friends" and including quips about the house's Spanish-mission style and the distinctly modern Swedish sunroom that was largely decorated by his wife. If it is a cool, rainy night, he would compare the evening to a glorious summer night in Sweden.

The ambassador would often acknowledge special guests during his toasts, such as a Supreme Court justice or a senator or a State Department official. He circulated around the residence during receptions, dipping into conversations, perhaps lingering longer if there was some business to transact. If he wanted to discuss a difficult or contentious matter with a guest, he was careful not to bring it up in front of the person's spouse.

"If the occasion seems right and the other person is willing to go for it, I go for it," he said. "But sometimes I make it a point not to raise an issue, even if it's in the back of my mind. It might not be the right time."

The ambassador draws energy from social events. "I could be dead tired but when I enter a room I take on life. I put a certain emphasis into it," he said. "When I'm the host I want to make sure the room buzzes," he said.

Eliasson is convinced that social diplomacy is an integral part of the broader diplomatic craft. "There is a very strong impression that diplomats have a very luxurious life. But it's very hard work," Eliasson said. "A lot of people think diplomacy is just cocktail parties and receptions," Eliasson said. "I have the greatest respect for these things. In fact, I actually like them. But if that's all you do, you're not taken seriously. You can't divorce social life and substance. You can't just be a socialite. You should be a good speaking partner. You should contribute something. There has to be a certain elegance," he said.

⌘ V ⌘

Parties are important in Washington diplomacy because they often give the ambassador an easy pretext to meet someone he wants to meet or to discuss some business. But many times it's just a matter of creating goodwill—which might be helpful to draw upon sometime in the future.

"The ambassador is very good at these parties," said Beth Jones, a former State Department official. "He's polished without being pompous or boring."

⌘ VI ⌘

A reception Eliasson hosted in the early spring of 2004 illustrates how the ambassador built, sustained, and expanded his network during his Washington years. The occasion was a dinner at his elegant Nebraska Avenue residence for Hans Blix, the former chief United Nations weapons inspector.

Blix is a fellow Swede, a friend, and something of a mentor of Eliasson's. Blix is also a rock star in Sweden, celebrated as a statesman who spoke the truth to American power about Iraq's alleged weapons of mass destruction programs. But Blix is very unpopular with the Bush administration; they clashed repeatedly—and publicly—about his inspection work in the run-up to the American-led invasion of Iraq in 2003.

On this night, Blix is in Washington on the final leg of a book tour in the United States in which he has been blasting the administration about its policy toward Iraq. It's been difficult to turn on a cable news show this week and not see Blix scorching the administration for rushing into the war with Iraq before carefully assessing intelligence or allowing the inspections process to work. Blix's message has been simple: when it comes to Iraq the Bush team has been careful not to confuse itself with facts or evidence.

But Eliasson's challenge is complex: to host a party that is respectful of Blix without bashing the Bush administration, which he works with every day. Staging such an event requires tact and creativity. For a man who has worked in war zones in Somalia, Sudan, and the Balkans, who negotiated a truce in the brutal war in Nagorno-Karabakh, who spent more than twenty-five hours in direct and intense talks with Saddam Hussein in the 1980s, including harrowing negotiations in Saddam's presidential palaces, arranging a Washington dinner is a distinctly doable deal.

But Eliasson approached the dinner with his trademark penchant for detail and caution. First, he decided not to have a full-scale bash, opting instead for a small dinner with a group of policy experts. Then the ambassador carefully assembled the guest list with the help of Stone and Lundkvist.

"I had to make a strategic choice when I arranged the guest list," he recalls. "Invite the administration? No. Invite the Democratic opposition? Also no. I wanted distinguished people from the academic and think tank world who are interested in arms control and weapons of mass destruction.

"I wanted to play it right. I didn't want to exploit Hans. He's not a representative of Sweden. He's a retired international civil servant. He has a right to his opinions. It is good he's been vindicated on so much. I defended him publicly and was even ridiculed. He's been good for Sweden," the ambassador said.

The ambassador's guests included former Defense Secretary Robert McNamara; former White House counselor Lloyd Culter; Georgetown University Dean Bob Gallucci; Jim Steinberg and Ivo Daalder from the Brookings Institution; David Calleo from the Johns Hopkins University School of Advanced International Studies (SAIS); Chester Crocker from Georgetown University; Jessica Einhorn, the dean of SAIS; Robert Einhorn, an arms control expert at the Center for Strategic and International Studies; Egypt's Ambassador Nabil Fahmy; and Walter Pincus, the *Washington Post's* intelligence reporter. Stone greeted guests at the door of the residence and then ushered them into a large reception room where the ambassador introduced visitors individually to Blix.

One of the requirements of diplomacy, the ambassador believes, is perfecting the art of the forty-five-second conversation. And judging from his work tonight, Eliasson has this skill down cold. He greets all guests by name, introduces them to Blix, and orchestrates a brief exchange. The conversation unfolds for about a minute, and then Eliasson politely turns his attention to the next guest.

As guests mingle under a massive floor-to-ceiling tapestry of King Gustav III, Eliasson calls the evening to order, urging everyone to take a quick tour of the adjacent sunroom, quipping that humanity is divided between those who love and those who detest the ultramodern room. He then leads the guests into his dining room where they sit at four tables under a magnificent cut-crystal baroque chandelier.

Eliasson relishes the role of master of ceremonies and pulls it off with uncommon skill, employing healthy doses of wit, quips, self-deprecation, and flattery. "All of you could be guests of honor at the Swedish embassy," he says, noting that about half the people at the dinner are in Blix's book index—the Washington measure of significance and heft. "And we're very glad you're here tonight," Eliasson says turning to Blix. He gives a warm introduction to Blix and describes how his career has intersected with the careers of Blix and his wife, who is a Swedish diplomat.

Blix, a constitutional lawyer and former director general of the Atomic Energy Agency, then gives a long and methodical monologue leavened with a sprinkling of arms control humor. Blix summarizes his career and the history of the world's effort to disarm Iraq.

"We were there to perform effective and professional inspections, not to humiliate or harass or provoke Iraq," Blix says of his Iraq venture at the end of 2002 and in early 2003. I have my doubts that Saddam Hussein was in an aggressive mode in 2002," he adds.

After Blix's twenty-minute overview of the Iraq inspection debacle, Eliasson solicits questions from the guests and Blix responds to several gentle queries about his strategy and tactics. Eliasson asks Blix to comment on one of the great imponderables: whether his inspection work, if allowed to continue, could have led to the removal of Saddam's regime without a war. Blix, using a complex rhetorical formulation, offers a clear answer: probably.

As the questions wind down, Eliasson whispers to Bob Gallucci who had worked with Blix during his time as an arms control negotiator in the Clinton administration. Eliasson invites Gallucci to make a statement or pose a question. At first hesitant, Gallucci notes that he and Blix sometimes differed when they worked together long ago, but adds that Blix has had an important and successful career—and has often been right on important issues.

Eliasson ends the dinner with high praise for Blix, complimenting him for "your magnanimity, your evenhandedness, your fairness, your gentility." There is warm applause.

As guests file out the front door of the residence, most a little wobbly from the generous servings of red wine, the ambassador shakes hands and says to nearly everyone: "Wasn't it an interesting night?"

But his night isn't over.

When the last of his guests have lumbered off, Eliasson retreats to his library, yanks off his tie, slides into an oversized red chair, and settles down for a couple of hours of work. This is the less glamorous side of diplomacy.

He was preparing to give a lecture later in the week on mediation to a group of graduate students at Johns Hopkins and was trying to distill forty years of experience into a forty-minute lecture.

Eliasson will also host a charity event at his residence for the Appleseed Foundation, which he needs to bone up on. He will make remarks at the reception and wants to make sure he fully understands what the foundation does and how it works. And then there are cables from Stockholm to read, memos from his staff to review, and various Swedish newspapers to browse through.

This is another day and night of Washington diplomacy for Jan Eliasson.

CHAPTER 8

The Colony

Eliasson speaking at a midsummer party at his residence

◈ I ◈

On a warm Sunday morning in June, Ambassador Eliasson and his press counselor, Claes Thorson, drove to Pennsville, New Jersey, about ninety minutes from Washington, so the ambassador could participate in a ceremony hosted by the local Swedish American community. Eliasson worked hard at developing relationships with Americans of Swedish ancestry, a group he teasingly called "my colony."

On this day, he's attending a ceremony in which a monument will be unveiled to commemorate the New Sweden colony that flourished from 1638 to 1655. A student of history, Eliasson is interested in New Sweden, the first permanent European colony in the Delaware valley. He is especially proud of the peaceful relationship between Swedish settlers and the Lenni Lenape Indians. He's had several meetings with Lenape leaders and is even trying to find linguistic experts in Stockholm to help them recover parts of their language.

Eliasson looks remarkably rested, given that he was out dancing until the wee hours of the morning. The ambassador's wife, Kerstin, has returned from Sweden to Washington for a long weekend. The Eliassons hosted a dinner the night before as part of the Washington Opera Ball. Later they joined hundreds of guests for dessert and dancing at the British embassy.

As the ambassador's limousine pulls out of his driveway, Eliasson is on the phone to Stockholm, speaking to various officials about a letter of condolence that is being drafted to Nancy Reagan. Former President Ronald Reagan died the previous day and Eliasson is offering ideas on the language for Sweden's letter of sympathy. He is also discussing who Sweden should send to attend the Reagan funeral.

The ambassador slips into an intense mood as he tries to get these matters resolved. But once he has offered his ideas, he loosens up. He sprawls in the backseat, putting his legs on the seat across from him, reading the Sunday *New York Times* and chatting with Thorson and myself.

As his car approaches Pennsville, the ambassador shifts back into a serious, intense mood. He checks his handwritten notes to review whom he is going to meet and what he's going to say at the ceremony.

If ambassadors are a dime a dozen in Washington, they are a big deal outside the Beltway. And today Eliasson is visiting a community of Swedish Americans who are eager to see the ambassador. He's about to be treated like a conquering hero.

As he arrives in Pennsville, the ambassador jumps out of the car and strides immediately toward the waterfront festival at River Beach Park. The organizers approach Eliasson and within seconds he is transformed from a limousine diplomat to a Clintonesque politician.

This afternoon he is a flurry of focused, amiable energy, as he shakes hands, hugs acquaintances, poses for pictures, holds babies, and dutifully gazes at a replica of a Viking ship. Eliasson prowls along the waterfront for half an hour before heading into the restaurant at the Riverview Inn for a buffet lunch and a dance program. He seems deeply moved by a dance routine by some Lenape dancers that emphasizes the unity of mankind.

The ceremony shifts back outside to the River Beach Park along the Delaware River. The ambassador sits in the front row and smiles through a long program, packed with historical reenactments, speeches by local politicians, and wordy proclamations.

Eliasson then is called to the stage for his remarks and takes over the program. He notes there are about ten million Americans with some family connections to Sweden and only nine million Swedes.

"I sometimes joke with the prime minister that I have more constituents than he has," Eliasson says. Then he launches into one of his trademark speeches to the Swedish American community.

"We have several identities," he declares. "I think it is a mistake to think of identity as singular. When we think of identity as plural something wonderful happens. We can't divide humanity into us and them. Because we are all the same. We belong together.

"We must be aware of roots, but also aware of wings. It's important to strike that balance in life between roots and wings. To take up the best of the past, learn from the past, live intensely in the present, but also have dreams and aspirations for the future."

As the program ends, much of the audience swarms toward Eliasson. He poses for pictures, signs autographs, and lingers—clearly basking in the connection and the adulation. This is the ambassador as star.

❧ II ❧

Some ethnic communities are large, colorful, and powerful. Others are small, silent, and politically and culturally insignificant. The Swedish American community rests between those two extremes. It's medium sized, prosperous, and connected to the "home country," albeit in a quiet, unspectacular way.

The era of mass Swedish immigration to the United States was between 1850 and 1930 when more than 1.3 million Swedes arrived. Minnesota received more Swedish immigrants than any other state. The peak of Swedish immigration to the United States was 1910. Chicago was the largest Swedish settlement in the United States, but these immigrants did not shape the city's ethnic population the same way they did in Minneapolis or Saint Paul.

Of the ten million Americans who claim Swedish ancestry, there are large concentrations in Minnesota, Wisconsin, New York, and Chicago, but also in places you might not guess: Seattle, San Francisco, Los Angeles, and Austin.

Eliasson made it a serious goal to get to know and to energize the members of this community. He sought out leading members of his colony, such as Chief Justice William Rehnquist who was a frequent guest at embassy events. Rehnquist was proud of his Swedish ancestry, and Eliasson reached out to him in an inviting yet discreet way. The ambassador hosted Rehnquist's eightieth birthday party at his residence and invited the chief justice to the embassy's Santa Lucia Christmas party and to its annual dinner for American Nobel Laureates.

He worked with prominent Swedish Americans to get better plugged in to American political life. For example, Sweden's consul general in San Francisco, Barbro Osher, introduced him to two important friends of hers: House Democratic Leader Nancy Pelosi and former Senate Democratic Leader Tom Daschle.

In working with the Swedish American community, Eliasson selected Thorson, his press counselor, to be the chief contact person. Sweden has two full consulates in the United States that serve the Swedish American community. One consulate is in New York and one is in Los Angeles. A third Swedish consulate will be opened in Houston in 2007.

The ambassador also used the embassy's thirty honorary consulates to keep in touch with the community. These consulates are spread across the country and are coordinated by the embassy.

Eliasson used several large organizations as a vehicle to reach the Swedish American community. The Swedish Council of America acts as an umbrella group for about three hundred fifty affiliated Swedish American organizations with tens of thousands of members. Created more than thirty years ago, it is the central entity that helps the various organizations preserve and enrich the Swedish heritage in North America and support a strong relationship between Sweden and America. The Swedish Council gives over $25,000 in grants to projects that preserve and promote the Swedish American heritage in North America. It also runs several award programs including the Great Swedish Heritage Award, America's Swede of the Year, and the Swedish Council of America Awards of Merit. Eliasson was named 2005 Swede of the Year. The Swedish Council also hosts a biannual conference about Swedish America.

The Swedish American community helps fund four major museums: the American Swedish Historical Museum, the American Swedish Institute, the Nordic Heritage Museum, and the Swedish American Museum Center.

The Swedish American community helps support several colleges that emphasize their Swedish roots, including Augustana College in Illinois, Bethany College in Kansas, Gustavus Adolphus College in Minnesota, and California Lutheran University in California.

Eliasson and the embassy also tapped into the energy of the Swedish Women's Educational Association (SWEA), a worldwide organization established in the United States in 1979, which awards scholarships, builds networks, and promotes the role of women.

Also the Swedish American Chamber of Commerce, which is composed of a national office and nineteen regional offices, hosts a popular trade show where Swedish and American firms explore partnerships and investment opportunities. Additionally, the embassy works with the Swedish American Chamber of Commerce to host an annual golf outing every fall that often includes a reception at the ambassador's residence.

Herbert Rambo, head of the Swedish Colonial Society in New Jersey, says Eliasson quickly grasped that there are three distinctive Swedish American communities in the United States and tapped into each. One group comprises recent immigrants and Swedish citizens living in the United States. They tend to closely identify with Swedish culture and most of them are fluent in English as well as Swedish. This group has always worked closely with Sweden's embassy in Washington.

The second group comes from the original Swedish community in the United States. the antient Rambo says these are the fourteenth- and fifteenth-generation Americans whose ancestry and ties to the New Sweden Colony make them distinctive in both the United States and Sweden.

The largest segment of the Swedish American community is the second and third generation of the great Swedish immigration of the nineteenth and twentieth centuries. Some of these people speak Swedish, but their connection to Sweden fades with each passing year. Rambo says that Eliasson was especially effective in reaching out to this group, helping revitalize their connection to the mother country.

"I can't remember a time when the embassy was more engaged with Swedish America than it was during Jan Eliasson's tenure. His steady cultivation of all parts of Swedish America resulted in people liking him. He was interested in them and they were pleased," Rambo said.

"With all his bridge building, Jan Eliasson was able to combine personal involvement, a heavy schedule of visits, and personal charm to create opportunities to spread the views of the Swedish government to a wider audience. It seems Ambassador Eliasson was everywhere," he added.

Jan and Kerstin Ealisson hosting their Santa Lucia party

ৡৡ III ৡৡ

Eliasson said he decided even before arriving in Washington that making contact with the Swedish American community was one of his top priorities and that he wanted to do so in a way that built on important traditions, such as Santa Lucia and Midsummer, the Christmas and summer holidays, but was also creative and oriented toward the future.

Santa Lucia is the Swedish holiday before Christmas in which young girls dressed in white and with candles in a crown that is placed on their heads serenade guests at the ambassador's residence. Eliasson made special efforts to ensure this event went smoothly, even to the point of being involved in the selection of songs and the pace of the procession.

"It is our protest movement against the darkness," Eliasson said of Lucia. The ambassador hosted this party in two stages—an early evening reception for the embassy staff and then a later one for other guests of the embassy.

Lucia was an Italian saint who was martyred for having become a Christian. The Lucia tradition, experts say, was brought to Sweden by Christian Vikings one thousand years ago.

Midsummer is a holiday around the summer solstice that celebrates the Swedish summer during which the sun almost never sets. Eliasson would invite up to eight hundred guests to the residence for this holiday. They would gather in the embassy's massive back lawn and enjoy Swedish snacks and games.

Eliasson and previous Swedish ambassadors used these as the two pillar events for the Swedish American community and friends of the embassy. But the ambassador tried to go beyond these two celebrations to find new ways to stimulate the community. His interest in the New Sweden colony and its historic relationship with the Lenape Indians is an example of this.

"One of my basic convictions is the embassy needs to work as a catalyst, we have to get other forces to work in our interests, to help us convey what we want to project. I think the Swedish American community has been an untapped resource," the ambassador said.

"I put a strong emphasis on reaching out to this community. I try to speak at major events. I try to speak clearly and make a strong statement. If it comes from the ambassador, the message gets a certain hearing."

Eliasson tried to make inroads with the younger generation, finding ways to make their Swedish heritage more relevant. He summarized his appeal by his frequent use of the "roots and wings" metaphor, which encouraged Swedish Americans to celebrate where their families came from, honor this tradition, but continue to look to the future.

"As I travel to events around the country I've noticed the median age is pretty high. It's very important that the next generation of Swedish Americans has a sense of their background and knowledge of their culture. That requires extra effort. I've made that a theme: to make sure we connect with young people."

But some question if Eliasson's appeal to younger Swedish Americans is a realistic objective. One Swedish diplomat who was based in the United States for many years said that for almost all people their connection with their ethnic roots only becomes relevant and important as they grow older.

"It's like Russian churches. They are always filled with old women. They always have [been]. They always will."

Eliasson decided not to create a high-level advisory group of Swedish Americans to formally advise him on issues of importance to this community. He said this was just make-work and would accomplish little.

"I'm not in favor of creating artificial structures that are not needed. Swedes and Swedish Americans are very organized people. They create organizations that we can work with," he said.

Eliasson also decided not to try to create a "Friends of Sweden" caucus in Congress, saying support for Sweden was strong on Capitol Hill and didn't require a new organization to sustain.

Eliasson said he viewed his role with the Swedish American community as that of a conductor, presiding over the colony and speaking during important events and occasions.

"It's very important, but I can't afford to spend a lot of time on it. My work in Washington is all absorbing. And my main task is to be a link to the American administration and the Congress and political life in Washington."

❧ IV ❧

Siri Eliason, chairman of the board of directors of the Swedish Council of America, said the ambassador's work with the Swedish American community has been significant.

"Ambassador Eliasson has been the best ambassador I've ever seen regarding work with the Swedish American community. He really cares about Swedish Americans, understands their history and heritage. He understands the hardships endured by many of those who came here. He went all out in supporting this community. He talked about things in such a compelling, emotional way. He reached people's heartstrings."

Barbro Osher, the consul general in San Francisco, said the ambassador connected with the Swedish American community wherever he went.

"Jan's totally engaging, well informed, incredibly skilled socially. You don't find someone more professional than Jan. He reached out to the Swedish American community with great skill. He's a wonderful speaker, he hits all the right notes, makes all the right points."

CHAPTER 9

Penetrating the Government

Eliasson at the U.S Capitol

§ª **I** §ª

It's a busy spring afternoon on Capitol Hill and Jan Eliasson has found one
of the few quiet places in Congress's sprawling complex of buildings: a hearing by the European subcommittee of the House International Relations
Committee on developments in northern Europe.

83

Relentlessly punctual, Eliasson enters Room 2200 of the Rayburn House Office Building about fifteen minutes before the hearing is set to begin. He circulates around the light-blue-walled room, talking with committee staffers, officials from the State Department, several aides from the Swedish embassy, and a few journalists.

For reasons of protocol and tradition, it's very unusual for an ambassador from another country to testify before the U.S. Congress. But Eliasson and Vygaudas Ušackas, Lithuania's ambassador to the United States have been invited to testify on developments in northern Europe and specifically on a new initiative that involves the United States and the nations of the Baltic region.

Heather Conley, the deputy assistant secretary of state for European and Eurasian affairs, is the administration's witness. Only the chairman of the subcommittee, Republican Douglas Bereuter, and Representative Robert Wexler, the top Democrat on the subcommittee, are attending the hearing. The panel's dozen other members have found other things to do.

The topic under consideration is not, shall we say, a media-enticing event. There are no TV cameras in sight and most attending the hearing are young congressional staffers or analysts from research groups that follow northern Europe.

Bereuter, the subcommittee chairman, calls the hearing to order, noting the rarity of ambassadors testifying before Congress. He then outlines the central elements of the e-Pine program—an acronym for Enhanced Partnership in Northern Europe. He says that the State Department launched the Northern European Initiative (NEI) in 1997 in an effort to help Estonia, Latvia, and Lithuania fully integrate into the community of European democracies. These three Baltic states joined NATO in 2004 and the same three plus Poland were to enter the European Union in about two weeks from the hearing, May 1, 2004. Bereuter says that the State Department has recast the NEI into the Enhanced Partnership in Northern Europe, which was formally unveiled by Conley the previous fall.

After Wexler makes a few introductory comments, the lawmakers invite Conley to testify. She provides some of the program's history and places it in a broader political and security context. Conley, who's served as a top diplomat for European affairs since September 2001, explains to the panel that the Nordic/Baltic region comprises Iceland, Norway, Denmark, Sweden, Finland, Estonia, Latvia, and Lithuania. Six of the eight are members of NATO; six will be members of the European Union after its coming expansion.

"The Nordic/Baltic region is truly a region, a group of countries who share geography and interest in ideas and that build up structures that enhance their cooperation," she says. Conley says that e-Pine was created to promote security, healthy societies and healthy neighbors, and vibrant economies in the region.

Eliasson and Ambassador Ušackas are then invited to present their views. While Eliasson has spent little of his time in Washington attending congressional hearings, he has watched enough C-SPAN to understand the ritual and handle the event smoothly. State Department officials recommended Eliasson and Ušackas as witnesses to the committee because both are seen as forceful, articulate, polished—and enthusiastic supporters of the program. A smooth public presence, Eliasson hits all the right notes. He praises Bereuter for his work on European matters and notes the veteran lawmaker is set to retire in a few weeks.

"I would like to commend you for your leadership of this committee. You have always been a champion of transatlantic relations," Eliasson tells Bereuter. Trying to put the hearing in a broader context, Eliasson cites the progress that has taken place in the Nordic/Baltic world since 1990 and praises the United States for developing constructive policies toward the region.

"Like our own programs, e-Pine builds on previous efforts and experiences. Our region did not turn into an area of good news in a world of bad news by accident. The Nordic countries have had extensive cooperation with the Baltic countries even before they regained their independence," he says. He notes that from 1990 to 2003, Sweden provided more than $500 million in bilateral assistance to the Baltics as well as in-kind assistance in the form of military equipment.

Eliasson praises Conley for helping shape e-Pine and touts in a careful, subtle way Sweden's role in developing the program, which involves regular meetings and policy discussions.

"We feel that Sweden made some modest contributions to the development of the program. In early 2003, we handed over a food-for-thought on opportunities for future cooperation with the United States in the Baltic Sea region. This paper landed at the right time with the process under way in the State Department in Heather Conley's bureau. We are happy to note that some of our ideas were well received and are reflected in the e-Pine structure," he adds.

Speaking with care, Eliasson makes it clear that Sweden doesn't want the program to be changed into a more structured, bureaucratic program. But he also signals that Sweden wants the e-Pine countries to place much greater emphasis on reaching out to other struggling nations in eastern Europe.

"Sweden believes that the most important areas to focus on are the countries neighboring the e-Pine area to the east. This means in particular Belarus,

Ukraine, Moldova, and also Russia and the former Soviet republics of the Caucasus and Central Asia.

"We do not think that e-Pine should concern itself primarily with projects exclusively within the e-Pine area, but rather with promoting cooperation and tackling issues of concern to all of us, including our eastern neighbors."

Eliasson concludes his remarks, and during the subcommittee's question and answer session he stays on message regarding the promise of e-Pine. But he also presents Sweden's views on other sensitive issues, including reform in Russia, problems in Belarus, human trafficking in the region, and environmental challenges facing the Baltic Sea. He argues that while Sweden supports a stronger European Union this does not suggest that it wants to de-emphasize its relationship with the United States.

As the session ends, Eliasson walks to the dais and banters with Bereuter and his staff. He tells the lawmaker that he would like to host a lunch for him before he retires from Congress and invites him to visit him sometime in his summer home in Gotland.

The hearing is not an electric event and generates no press coverage in the United States. But it's been a successful, albeit low-key, afternoon for the ambassador.

He presented Sweden's views before an important congressional committee, solidified his relationship with a key State Department official, and participated in a Washington event that signals to Sweden's foreign ministry in Stockholm that he is respected and consulted in the United States. Not bad for a few hours' work.

৯৯ II ৯৯

For all the changes in the job of the modern ambassador, the envoy's central responsibility is clear and unchanged: to represent your home government to your host government. For Eliasson, this required knowing the pivotal personalities in the administration and Congress; understanding how policies were developed, when they were developed, who developed them; and the best way for Sweden to present its views.

Few ambassadors in Washington have anything more than brief and highly irregular meetings with the American president. If they are fortunate, they may chat with him once or twice a year during receptions or in receiving lines.

Ambassadors also typically have relatively few encounters with the secretary of state or the national security advisor. They may see the secretary at several social events that are held for the entire diplomatic corps, such as a Fourth of July reception at the State Department where they can watch the fireworks on the National Mall, or a Christmas reception at Blair House. Ambassadors also are hosted at a State Department buffet before they are taken to hear the State of the Union speech in January.

Most of their work with the administration takes place several levels below the secretary of state or NSC director. Eliasson presented his credentials to President Bill Clinton in September of 2000, the final months of the Clinton administration. He later met with him at a reception honoring American winners of the various Nobel prizes. Eliasson had met Clinton before, when he had served as Sweden's deputy foreign minister. Eliasson had a good relationship with Secretary of State Madeleine Albright and a long-standing friendship with her deputies, Strobe Talbott and Tom Pickering.

In addition to larger receptions, Eliasson met with Bush each year in connection with the Nobel awards. In late fall of 2001, Eliasson spoke at a White House ceremony after Bush did, commemorating the hundredth anniversary of the Nobel prizes. Eliasson and his wife were asked by Rice, then the NSC chief, to join Bush and his wife at the head of the receiving line for the Nobel laureates.

Eliasson was fortunate that less than six months after arriving in Washington, Sweden assumed the presidency of the European Union. Sweden held that six-month rotating presidency from January 1 to July 1, 2001. During that time Eliasson made high-level contacts with the Bush administration, which a new ambassador, especially from a middle-sized country, would be unlikely to make. Additionally, the new administration was just assuming power and was in an outreach mode.

Eliasson had extensive dealings with Powell and his deputy, Richard Armitage, and Rice and her deputy, Stephen Hadley, who later succeeded Rice as NSC chief. Using skills that were honed over his professional career, Eliasson found easy—but different—ways to connect with Powell and Rice and maintain the relationship he developed when he first arrived.

With Powell, the ambassador often enjoyed a pleasant banter, joking about the three Swedish things Powell most admired: Volvo, ABBA, and Anna Lindh. When Powell visited Gothenburg with Bush in June of 2001 as part of a meeting with American and EU leaders, Powell was taken on a tour of a Volvo factory where he observed crash tests and took a test drive. And when the musical *Mamma Mia* celebrating ABBA came to Washington, Eliasson lined up tickets and attended the show with Powell and Armitage.

With Rice, Eliasson was the respectful and cultured older colleague who shared her affinity for classical music. Rice and Kerstin Eliasson spoke easily and warmly about their shared love of music. The ambassador often gave Rice updates on his wife's favorite piano selections.

The ambassador had worked in the past with Rice's deputy secretary of state, Robert Zoellick. Shortly after Zoellick moved into his new job, Eliasson sent him a congratulatory note and a book about Sweden's King Charles XII. Zoellick later thanked the ambassador for the book and invited Eliasson to his office at Foggy Bottom for a wide-ranging discussion of U.S.-EU relations, Russia, and other topics.

Eliasson also connected with the State Department's third-ranking official, the undersecretary of state for political affairs. The ambassador had an affable and easy relationship with Marc Grossman and his successor, Nicholas Burns. Eliasson was in touch with Grossman on September 11, 2001, to offer condolences and quietly gauge what was going on in the American government behind the scenes.

The ambassador's most frequent contacts at State focused on the bureau that oversaw the United States' relationship with Sweden: the Bureau of European and Eurasian affairs. Within that bureau, he kept in touch with the assistant secretary, at first Elizabeth Jones, who was then followed by Dan Fried. Eliasson also developed a good working relationship with Conley, the deputy assistant secretary. Jones said Eliasson was good humored, well informed, but also very serious.

"He was very good about explaining the situation in Sweden, what the domestic pressures were. He was always very professional," she said. "He was very easy to deal with. You could cover a wide range of subjects with him. He is very easy to talk to. You could explain things to him candidly and directly. He understood how things work in Washington, and he was very clear about explaining the thinking in Stockholm."

Conley worked with Eliasson on a number of sensitive issues including the matter of the Swedish citizen detained at Guantanamo Bay as a prisoner. She called him when Swedish officials in Stockholm were highly critical of the United States. Both Lindh and Freivalds, the foreign ministers, were not reluctant to offer stinging remarks about various U.S. policies, which the American embassy in Stockholm reported back to Washington.

"I could call him and ask what does this mean, what is the context for this remark. I could be very honest with him and say we can solve this problem or your leadership can keep using sharp, public rhetoric and nothing will change," she said. Conley said the two often discussed the differing approaches to confronting terrorism. Swedish officials often said this battle had to be fought aggressively, but also with full respect for human rights.

American officials felt Sweden was not sufficiently vigilant in confronting potential terrorists living in Stockholm.

"When it comes to counterterrorism, Sweden is sometimes 'See no evil, hear no evil, speak no evil.' I made that point to Jan," Conley said. Conley said that Eliasson was successful because he had a shrewd understanding of how the American government operated and had a wide network of contacts he could tap into. Specifically, he understood that when it came to American policy in the Nordic-Baltic world most of the initiatives were formulated at the middle levels of the bureaucracy.

"Jan was very engaged and was not overly put off by protocol. When he needed an answer or information, he went to the person who had it. Some ambassadors won't deal with anyone below an assistant or deputy assistant level. Jan would dip in. He would call a desk officer," Conley said. "The ambassador used all the tools at his disposal to advance the bilateral relationship—social, cultural," she said. Eliasson was attentive and diligent and, on matters of real importance, she added, could be very aggressive.

"He worked incredibly hard every day. He understood the swirl of Washington. He understood that Washington doesn't speak with a monolithic voice. He had good bipartisan contacts across the government. He could get good, high-level appointments for visitors. When something was important he pushed very, very hard. He was relentless. But he also knew when to stop and back off."

Eliasson also developed a friendship with the director of the State Department's Protocol Office, Don Ensenat. The Protocol Office is the most direct point of contact for ambassadors to the American government. In this case, Ensenat is also a personal friend of Bush. The ambassador worked closely with Ensenat on several issues that were very important to Sweden, such as making sure a reception for Nobel laureates was placed on the White House's fall calendar.

Eliasson worked on some issues with the State Department's ambassador-at-large for war crimes issues, Pierre Prosper, and the ambassador-at-large for human trafficking, John R. Miller.

Eliasson developed a friendship with Andrew Natsios, head of the Agency for International Development, who is a close friend of the White House chief of staff, Andrew Card. Eliasson also worked closely with the NSC's leadership and staff, including the unit that dealt with European issues, which includes a special assistant to the president and senior director for European and Eurasian Affairs.

The ambassador carefully cultivated contacts at other agencies such as Commerce, Defense, Health and Human Services, Treasury, Homeland

Eliasson in the Oval Office during a visit by Sweden's prime minister

Security, and the U.S. Trade Representative's office. He became friends with
Samuel Bodman who was the Deputy Secretary at the Commerce and
Treasury departments before he became the Energy Secretary. Eliasson
began to focus on the Homeland Security department because it was an
important, new agency and was where lucrative contracts for Swedish firms
might be secured.

۞ III ۞

Eliasson says that in the fast-paced world of Washington diplomacy, there is
rarely time for "just checking in" phone calls or meetings with senior leaders
in the administration. The ambassador had frequent meetings at the State
Department and the White House to deal with bilateral issues or to plan for
visits to the United States by leaders from Sweden such as the prime minister, the foreign minister, other senior ministers, or parliamentarians. During
Eliasson's tenure he helped prepare for three meetings between Prime
Minister Göran Persson and Bush.

Bush visited Sweden in June 2001 when Sweden held the EU presidency. And he met with the Swedish prime minister twice in Washington—in December 2001 and April 2004. Working closely with the administration on the details of these visits was an important opportunity in several respects. The most important benefit was that it put Sweden on the policy radar in Washington, hopefully deepening U.S.-Swedish relations. A side benefit was that it gave Eliasson and his embassy staff a context to intensify contacts with the administration and Congress—contacts that Eliasson carefully nurtured.

Eliasson was one of thirteen ambassadors invited to Fort McNair to listen to Bush give a speech in 2005 about the universal nature of terrorism. And he was the only ambassador invited to the State Department for the swearing in of John Miller as ambassador-at-large for trafficking issues.

৯৯ **IV** ৯৯

Some ambassadors are fixtures on Capitol Hill, lobbying Congress for aid or weapons or trade agreements. Some embassies have large congressional liaison units to follow the work of Congress and anticipate the direction of key initiatives. Although the president is the dominant foreign policy actor, the Constitution delegates more specific foreign policy powers to Congress than the president. It has the power to declare war and to appropriate funds.

Eliasson was interested in Congress, generally followed what it was up to, and knew a number of important lawmakers. But Sweden had relatively little business pending before Congress. Because Sweden had few issues under debate by Congress, the ambassador had less of a reason to approach lawmakers. He developed some important relationships, but acknowledged that many of these happened by chance rather than strategy.

He had a cordial relationship with Senator Richard Lugar, chairman of the Senate Foreign Relations Committee, and Representative Tom Lantos, the top Democrat with the House International Relations Committee. But he had more remote connections with Senator Joe Biden, the top Democrat on the Senate Foreign Relations Committee, and Representative Henry Hyde, the chairman of the House International Relations Committee. He dealt with Senator Biden and Congressman Hyde, primarily through their top staffers.

He had some contacts with Senators Gordon Smith and George Allen, the former and current chairmen of the European Senate Foreign Relations Subcommittee. He had a close relationship with Senator Paul Sarbanes, a senior Democrat on the Foreign Relations panel.

He cultivated some senior staffers from the House and Senate side. Even as he entered his final year as ambassador, Eliasson said he wanted the embassy to develop a more systematic approach to cultivating Congress. But the ambassador chose not to follow the example of other countries and create a formal caucus in Congress, such as the Friends of Portugal, the Albanian Issues Caucus, the Baltic Caucus, the Congressional Azerbaijan Caucus, the Congressional Bangladesh Caucus, the Congressional Caribbean Caucus, the Congressional Caucus on Armenian Issues, the Congressional Caucus on Korea, the Congressional Caucus on Nigeria, the Friends of Switzerland Caucus, and the Senate Friends of Norway Caucus.

"I just don't think that's necessary for us. We have enough friends," Eliasson said.

CHAPTER 10

Working in the Idea Factory

Eliasson with Foreign Minister Freivalds after her presentation at the Center for Strategic and International Studies

❧ I ❧

When Laila Freivalds made her inaugural trip to Washington as foreign minister in February of 2004, her first meeting was at the State Department with Secretary of State Colin Powell. The meeting, which Jan Eliasson helped Freivalds prepare for, covered a wide range of issues: the U.S.-Sweden bilateral relationship, the pending expansion of NATO and the European Union, the Middle East, the Palestinian-Israeli conflict, Swedish participation in a Nordic provincial reconstruction team for Afghanistan, and developments in Russia.

After the meeting in Powell's office and a briefing with Powell outside the State Department, Freivalds, Eliasson, and several other Swedish diplomats were driven about a mile to their second appointment of the day: a seminar at the Center for Strategic and International Studies. Freivalds was the featured speaker hosted by CSIS's European Department.

Eliasson is a big believer in the importance of think tanks and was especially active in CSIS's European program. The ambassador believed this venue would give Freivalds an opportunity to discuss Sweden's foreign policy agenda with informed and influential foreign policy analysts with a special interest in European issues. Before the program began, Freivalds and Eliasson stepped into a hallway for a private conversation to review the session with Powell. Eliasson's assurances that it went well were a palpable relief for Freivalds.

In her remarks, which she read from a prepared text, not the preferred format in these sessions, the foreign minister discussed transatlantic relations on the eve of the enlargement of the European Union and NATO. She argued that a strong link between the United States and Europe is essential for Europe's security and development. A larger and stronger European Union, she said, would also be a more competent and dependable partner for the United States.

Freivalds said that there are many potential benefits of strong U.S.-EU cooperation, including stability in the Balkans, greater cooperation with independent states from the former Soviet Union, further economic and political integration of Russia into Euro-Atlantic structures, and a more comprehensive approach to bringing stability and prosperity to the Middle East.

Regarding the disagreements between many in Europe and the United States over the war in Iraq, Freivalds didn't mince words. "None of us has forgotten the disagreements in the run-up to the war in Iraq," she said. But she said it was time to move forward.

After her formal remarks, Freivalds fielded a wide range of questions about Sweden's stance on various economic, political, and security issues. Freivalds turned to Eliasson, who was seated near her at the head of a large rectangular table, for answers to several questions, including the status in the U.S. Congress of legislation to repeal an export subsidy that angered Europe and had been declared illegal by the World Trade Organization.

The group of about two dozen journalists, policy analysts, former government officials, and academic experts asked polite and informed questions.

Freivalds gained confidence as she came to understand this was an essentially benevolent audience.

The hour-long session did not buzz with electricity. There were no TV cameras covering Freivalds's talk; the seminar did not generate headlines or even make news in Washington. But it still achieved its central purpose: to allow Sweden's new foreign minister to meet some important analysts and articulate Sweden's view of the world to experts who will help shape the debate on American-European relations.

Freivalds left the CSIS seminar for a private meeting with former Secretary of State Madeleine Albright at the ambassador's residence and then a reception that evening where Powell stopped by.

৯৯ II ৯৯

Eliasson was an active, even eager, participant in Washington's think tank life. He believed it's an important way to meet key officials and to explore policy ideas in an often informal environment. The vibrancy of Washington's political debate is palpable in these research and talking shops.

"Think tanks are an indirect way of reaching Congress, the administration, and the media. It's an open environment where you can speak freely," he said.

Washington's think tank community is an especially congenial place for ambassadors such as Eliasson who don't have a stack of difficult bilateral issues facing them every day and who are interested in joining, and hopefully helping influence, the U.S. policy debate.

Think tanks are a pervasive feature of Washington's political culture. On any given day, there are several dozen think tank events in the city, many that focus on the issue of the day: the Iraq war, reconstruction in Afghanistan, the war on terror, tax reform, the Arab-Israeli dispute, or a Supreme Court vacancy. Think tank conferences are typically attended by journalists, congressional staffers, former government officials, current government officials, and aspiring government officials.

For Eliasson and other ambassadors, they are a congenial place for diplomats to learn about domestic debates, gauge the U.S. foreign policy mood, offer their government's perspective, and sometimes discuss their own ideas. While some dismiss Washington think tank life as little more than a predictable exchange of hot air, debates at think tanks have been crucial to policy decisions, ranging from the push to build a missile defense system in the United States to launching the war in Iraq and trying to overhaul Social Security. The shape of a new world order is being fashioned in Washington more than in any other capital, and think tanks, Eliasson believed, are where the policies and doctrines of international affairs are being formulated.

Think tanks are a boom industry in Washington. By one account, their numbers have mushroomed from seventy-three, decades ago, to more than three hundred today. Their experts testify before Congress, write op-eds, journal articles and books, and participate in the cable TV circuit. These think tanks are home to top policy experts, produce a raft of studies, monitor and contribute to the American policy debate, and often provide insights on what will happen in the future.

The term "think tank" comes from World War II military jargon for a secure room where plans and strategies could be discussed. First used in the 1950s it described contract research organizations, such as the Rand Corporation, that had been set up by the military after the war. By the 1960s think tank entered popular parlance to refer to various types of private research organizations.

The first generation of policy research institutions was founded around 1910 as an outgrowth of Progressive-era reforms. They were established and sustained by private philanthropy. A second generation of think tanks emerged in the twenty years or so after World War II to deal with Cold War security issues and America's domestic war on poverty. A third generation of smaller think tanks was founded in the 1970s and 1980s, largely as an outgrowth of ideological combat. Many of them are conservative and geared toward political activism rather than pure scholarship.

Eliasson viewed think tanks as an important resource to make contacts, pick up information, gauge the future direction of American foreign policy, outline Sweden's worldview, and explore ideas that had no official backing from his government.

"Think tanks are my secret love. By now, I think every think tank president is a personal friend. This is something I enjoy and love. They mean all sorts of things to me," he says. "I'm increasingly informal. I want to think aloud, break new ground. I think the greatest difference in Washington between now and the 1970s is the vitality of the think tanks."

The ambassador would often attend several think tank events a week and encourage his staff to attend them as well. He frequently attended sessions at the Aspen Institute, the Brookings Institution, the Carnegie Endowment for International Peace, SAIS, CSIS, the Center For Transatlantic Relations, the German Marshall Fund, the U.S. Institute of Peace, and the Woodrow Wilson Center.

Eliasson did not travel the think tank circuit randomly. He focused on programs and discussions that engaged his interest and that of his government. For example, the Swedish government and Eliasson were deeply interested in strengthening the link between the United States and Europe, the so-called transatlantic dialogue.

Eliasson also used think tank events to outline Sweden's far-ranging humanitarian agenda. This included Sweden's views on human rights, international law, development assistance, the trafficking of people, and prevention of conflicts. The ambassador said that in the rush of day-to-day dealings with the administration and Congress about specific problems there often was not the time or the opportunity to present his government's and his own views on these matters. Think tanks events were invaluable for this.

Finally, Eliasson used think tanks to participate in special research projects or task forces that gave Sweden exposure and the ambassador an opportunity to present the government's perspective and learn what important Americans were thinking. For example, he participated in sessions held by the Carnegie Endowment to draft a report confronting the proliferation of weapons of mass destruction. Interested in the topic but not expert about these issues, Eliasson asked the Foreign Ministry in Stockholm and his embassy staff in Washington to review draft documents and decide what issues and themes he should advance during meetings.

"I felt this was the best way to participate in and hopefully influence the debate on an important issue. But it was hard work. You can't just do the fun stuff," he said.

໖ III ໖

Jan Eliasson spent an entire Friday, January 14, 2005, serving as Sweden's prime minister. He enjoyed the job. Actually Eliasson spent the day at Washington's opulent Mandarin Hotel participating in a simulated exercise in which former heads of state and senior national leaders considered major issues facing the transatlantic community following a bioterrorist attack using a contagious disease.

The exercise was organized by the Center for Biosecurity of the University of Pittsburgh Medical Center and the Center for Transatlantic Relations of the Johns Hopkins University School for Advanced International Studies, and the Transatlantic Biosecurity Network, a group of medical, public health, and national security experts from the United States and ten European countries that have been meeting since early 2002.

In addition to Eliasson playing the Swedish prime minister, Madeleine Albright played president of the United States; Sir Nigel Broomfield, a former British ambassador, played the British prime minister; Gro Harlem Brundtland, former prime minister of Norway and former director general of the World Health Organization, played the WHO chief; Bernard Kouchner, member of the European parliament and former French minister of health, played the French president.

In the simulation, the participants are in Washington for a Transatlantic Security Summit. As they arrive, they discover that an epidemic of a contagious disease has broken out in several countries as a result of bioterrorist attacks. Before returning home to manage the crisis, the assembled leaders agreed to convene an emergency meeting to address the steps the transatlantic community could take to respond to the situation.

Eliasson and the other participants are asked to deal with the crisis in three exercise segments depicting world events as the problem unfolds. The goal is to highlight the major international issues likely to be associated with responses to deliberate epidemics and to provoke discussion about how to improve the transatlantic community's ability to prepare for and respond to bioattacks. Eliasson, as the Swedish prime minister, used the sessions to make the point that more global cooperation in almost all areas is needed. Albright, as the American president, was under great domestic political pressure to focus on helping Americans first and let the other countries fend for themselves.

"Madeleine, I understand your political problems, but I would hope you would use your political skills to get this message out to your countrymen: we cannot act in a way that divides us," Eliasson said as the Swedish prime minister. He also expressed frustration at the global community's lack of preparation to respond to surprise attacks.

"We are not prepared. We have to be careful about how we move ahead. This is a plan to create mass hysteria in the world and bring the world economy to a halt. We have responsibilities as leaders to lead sensibly. We may have to take a series of risks—we may even risk lives," he said during the exercise.

"We live in a time of new threats. And we need new responses. This shows we're not prepared. We don't have the right organizational structures for these responses, so we must be careful how we move ahead," he added.

The sessions were taped and were the subject of two shows by ABC's *Nightline* and a segment by the BBC.

The day-long session was productive for Eliasson on many levels. First, it freshened some important contacts for him, which included Albright and leaders in the think tank community. Second, it gave both him and Sweden

Eliasson awards Strobe Talbott, president of the Brookings Institution, with a Polar Star medal

good exposure in the United States and around the world in the various news accounts of the exercise. Without Eliasson's contacts in the think tank community, it is unlikely he would have been invited to play a prominent role in the exercise. Sweden would not be an automatic participant in a Transatlantic Security Summit. Finally, the ambassador found the sessions stimulating and troubling, and they persuaded him that Stockholm should take the issue of emergency response seriously. Eliasson urged his government to examine the case study carefully and discuss it during meetings of the European Union in Brussels. He vowed to bring up the problem in the UN when he went back to work there later in the year.

৯৯ IV ৯৯

Eliasson said Washington's think tank community is substantially more visible and important than it was when he was in America in the '70s. He believes his involvement with think tanks was a good use of his time.

"I don't go to a meeting unless I have an active interest. I'm rarely quiet. I think before I go. It provides us with a forum for exchanging ideas." He said these meetings often allowed him to float ideas—some of which were grabbed by others. "The main thing is that something happens. Sometimes it's better that someone else considers that it was their idea," he said.

Simon Serfaty, head of CSIS's Europe program, said Eliasson was perfect in these fora; he was knowledgeable, inquisitive, and open. "He has a genuine personal and intellectual curiosity that kept him unwilling to limit himself to what he knows or believes, and is always eager to learn more of what he does not know or might not believe," he said. "He attended many, many meetings I and some of my colleagues organized at CSIS, as a participant, discussant, speaker. Even on short notice he was well prepared, candid, and forceful.

"I remember all kinds of other meetings during which he actively helped the Washington community to not only spell E-U, but also appreciate Sweden's special role and specific interests in the EU, with Sweden as one of the few EU members that did not belong to NATO as well. Indeed, Jan Eliasson perfectly embodied personally the collective attitude of a country that still claims neutrality but never pretends to be neutral on any of the main issues of the moment."

Richard Solomon, president of the U.S. Institute of Peace, said Eliasson sometimes attended workshops and seminars unannounced and plunged right into the discussions. "Jan's intellectually lively and engaged. He's almost the only ambassador who regularly showed up at our programs. He would come down to our workshops and seminars. He's rather unique in that he is willing not to be constrained by protocol," he said.

CHAPTER 11

The Road Trip

Eliasson holds a young boy at a festival hosted by Swedish-Americans

⚘ I ⚘

On a beautiful, sun-splashed spring day in Madison, Wisconsin, Jan Eliasson strolls into the spacious main lounge at the university's student union with a broad smile on his face. The room is packed with more than a hundred college students, professors, and middle-aged men and women with a distinctly Scandinavian look.

Eliasson enters the lounge with the Norwegian ambassador, Knut
Vollebaek, and the dean of the university's international studies department,
Gilles Bousquet. He sizes up the audience, gazes out a window at a large lake,
and looks very content.

The two ambassadors were on the final day of a three-day midwestern
tour. That morning's talk at the University of Wisconsin was on "Conflict
Resolution: Swedish and Norwegian Experiences."

Eliasson and Vollebaek decided to travel to the heart of Scandinavian
America in the spring of 2005 to celebrate a centennial. They teasingly disagreed on precisely what they were commemorating. Norway left its union
with Sweden in 1905 after about ninety years. So Norway decided to celebrate
2005 as the one hundredth anniversary of its independence from Sweden. The
Swedes, aware of Norway's plans, decided to participate fully in the occasion—
by recasting it and declaring it as a stirring example of the peaceful resolution
of conflict. After all, despite some threats and harsh words, Sweden allowed
Norway to leave the union without waging a war to halt the dissolution.

The two governments held joint events in Sweden and Norway in the
spring of 2005. Eliasson and Vollebaek organized a road trip to the epicenter
of the Scandinavian community in the United States: Wisconsin and
Minnesota.

The two ambassadors are good friends with a teasing rivalry that Swedes
and Norwegians seem to eagerly participate in. This trip was an opportunity
to get out of Washington, see what a different part of the country is thinking and saying, and to reconnect with important constituencies.

Like most successful road shows, this one was tested at home before the
two ambassadors traveled to the Midwest. A few weeks earlier, Eliasson and
Vollebaek participated in a seminar in Washington called "The Triumph of
Reason," which was hosted by the Alliance for International Conflict
Prevention and Resolution. The seminar, held at the Mayflower Hotel, celebrated "the blood that was not spilled in two potentially violent
separations"—Norway's secession from Sweden and the amiable divorce of
the Slovak and Czech republics.

At that conference, Eliasson and Vollebaek shared a stage and broadly
agreed on the progression of events that led to the end of Norway's union with
Sweden. Vollebaek believes the threat of Swedish force to keep Norway in the
union was more serious than Eliasson does, but they differ in an amiable and
respectful way. The Washington seminar gave the two ambassadors a chance to
test how they could succinctly summarize the past and use that as a foundation to talk about the present and the future.

Eliasson and Vollebaek began their midwestern trip with a Wednesday afternoon flight from Washington to Minneapolis. They attended a VIP reception at the Minnesota governor's mansion and then were taken to the Radisson Plaza Hotel for a private dinner and a briefing from the Swedish and Norwegian honorary consuls about the final schedule for the coming days.

On Thursday, Eliasson and Vollebaek had an early breakfast and then were driven to the studio of Minnesota Public Radio for an hour-long appearance on the *Midmorning Show*. Apparently for the people of Minnesota, 9 a.m. is midmorning. After the radio show, the two ambassadors were driven to the *Minneapolis Star Tribune,* the largest newspaper in Minnesota, for a meeting with Jim Boyd, deputy editor of the editorial pages. After that interview, Eliasson and Vollebaek attended a luncheon with about one hundred business executives during which each ambassador gave a brief talk.

When the lunch ended at 2 p.m., the two ambassadors were driven to the Hubert H. Humphrey Institute for Public Affairs for the highest profile event of the trip: a presentation before about two hundred fifty guests, including former Vice President Walter Mondale. The event was taped by the local Public Broadcasting System station. After the speech and a reception hosted by the Norwegian Consulate the two ambassadors were taken to the airport for a 10 p.m. flight from the Twin Cities to Madison, Wisconsin.

They arrived in Madison at about 11 p.m. Thursday night and were back at work by 8:30 Friday morning for a meeting with Wisconsin's lieutenant governor. Eliasson was dressed in a blue suit with a red tie and pocket hankie—Norway's national colors, he points out, a gesture to congratulate Norway on its centennial of independence.

After some introductory remarks by Dean Bousquet, Eliasson was invited to the podium to begin the program. He exulted about the beauty of the Big Ten university's lakefront campus in springtime. "What a wonderful campus you have. It must be great to be here," he said.

Eliasson then paid tribute to the Scandinavian immigrants who helped build Wisconsin and other parts of the United States. "I'm in awe of our forefathers," he said. Then, continuing to touch all the bases, he praised the University of Wisconsin's academic tradition, which includes a diverse student body comprising dozens of nationalities. The single most tangible way to begin addressing the world's problems, he said, is a "massive exchange of students."

Then moving to the theme of his talk, Eliasson described one of the central themes of Sweden's diplomatic history and his own career—mediation and conflict prevention. "I'm almost obsessed by the idea of prevention," he said to an attentive audience. "We've said 'never again' far too often, never again after Cambodia, never again after Rwanda, never again after Srebrenica, and now the Sudan."

As a contrast to the grim confrontations that continue to rage around the world, Eliasson celebrated the openness and serenity of the Scandinavian world. He warned that nations such as Sweden and Norway cannot be indifferent bystanders in a world of suffering. But he said there are lessons for the world about Nordic comity and serenity.

"When you cross the borders in the Nordic region, it's a positive. And if you have positive relations with your neighbors you almost always become an internationalist," he argued. He praised the warm relations now in place between Norway and Sweden, and credits them in part to the skillful negotiators of 1905, who found a way for a peaceful and respectful separation.

"The only competition we now have, apart from hockey and skiing, is how good we are in development assistance and conflict prevention. That's a wonderful form of competition," he said.

Vollebaek's talk echoed similar themes and then the two ambassadors invited questions from the audience. A cascade of articulate, even penetrating questions, gushed forth, challenging the diplomats to further describe their historical experiences and visions of the future.

A professor asked Eliasson a politely worded but very direct question about Sweden's role in World War II, specifically on several of its conciliatory policies toward Nazi Germany. "There are some aspects of Sweden's Second World War policies for which I'm ashamed," Eliasson said. But he adds that Sweden emerged from the war a soberer and more responsible nation.

"We are not conducting a policy of neutrality when it comes to values," he declared.

He skillfully recast a question about his views on the controversial nomination of John Bolton as the United States' representative at the United Nations to make a strong case for the United Nations. He noted several of its failures but cited the United Nation's accomplishments in Afghanistan and Lebanon and in protecting refugees and offering vaccinations to vulnerable populations.

"Why are things going pretty well in Afghanistan and not so good in Iraq? A lot of reasons: but the UN is one," he said.

When the dean tried to bring the session to a close, Eliasson politely dissented, basking in the curiosity and interest evident in the room. "This is fun. We can take some more questions."

After the session ended twenty minutes later, Eliasson and Vollebaek were surrounded by students and teachers who asked questions about diplomacy, current events, and careers in world affairs. The two ambassadors mingled and chatted for about a half an hour and then were off to lunch with Dean Bousquet before driving ninety miles to Milwaukee for a late-afternoon reception.

The two ambassadors headed up a receiving line at the elegant Milwaukee Club for more than an hour, bantering easily with a group of business leaders and Americans with Scandinavian blood. Maud Siljestrom, a buoyant Swedish American woman, gave Eliasson a book she wrote that outlines several walking tours of Stockholm.

With the conversation and drinks flowing, everyone was ushered into an adjacent wood-paneled reception room where the Swedish, Norwegian, and American flags were displayed.

Several local officials made brief remarks, followed by the two ambassadors. Eliasson received a large round of applause when a speaker mentioned that the Swedish ambassador will be the next president of the United Nation's General Assembly.

"I haven't been elected yet but it looks promising," he said in a well-practiced quip. "I'm now the only candidate." The room erupted into laughter and applause.

Eliasson concluded his brief talk by saying the world is facing historic crossroads where leaders will have to choose between multilateralism and unilateralism and between hope and fear.

"We are seeing a growing fear in the world. We need to instill a sense of hope, so we can come back to the great ideas we stand for—democracy, the free movement of people and ideas."

Vollebaek teased about how nice the warm reception feels for ambassadors who venture outside Washington. "We feel like we're so important," he joked, adding that diplomats in Washington have to compete for the fleeting attention of American leaders.

After Eliasson and Vollebaek spoke, Tom Barrett, Milwaukee's mayor and a former congressman, offered a simple statement of multilateral values that appeared to touch Eliasson.

"The UN has its challenges. But the world would be much worse off if we didn't have the UN. Your commitment to multilateralism is one I wish our country would return to. The world is better when we all work together."

Eliasson and Vollebaek left Milwaukee in the early evening, pleased with a successful trip. The events in Minnesota generated exceptional publicity. An hour on a popular radio show and the public seminar at the Humphrey Institute that was broadcast by the local PBS station allowed both ambassadors

Eliasson meets a modern-day Viking

to reach a wide audience. The *Minneapolis Star Tribune* article about their visit was brief, but concisely summarized the main themes of the two ambassadors' remarks. The *Milwaukee Journal Sentinel* had a question-and-answer article about the two ambassadors on the second page of the paper and included a photo of Vollebaek and Eliasson beaming.

ᚠ II ᚠ

Life on the road for an ambassador is easier than for the rest of us, but it's still grueling. Cars are usually waiting and comfortable arrangements have been made by others for lodging and meals. They travel like business executives, but this still means lines at the airport, cancelled flights, and missed connections. The days are busy, receptions crowded, and there is always the pressure to maintain a calm, upbeat, positive demeanor.

Being an ambassador on the road has its rewards and drawbacks. If ambassadors are a dime a dozen in Washington, they are at least minor celebrities when they travel to other parts of the country. They bring an impressive title, an intriguing professional background, and the cachet of representing a sovereign nation.

For many ambassadors, there is a compelling rationale to travel. Washington is not America; in fact, much of what happens in Washington is a reaction to demands and pressures emanating from the hinterland. Washington policy makers no longer defer to a small group of Wise Men for guidance on issues. For reasons of political survival, they pay attention to the feelings and demands of the rest of the country.

Additionally, while Washington may be the political capital of the United States, and even the world, it is not the only center of power in America. The industrial Midwest, Silicon Valley, the Pacific Northwest, California, and the Sunbelt are centers of business, and visits there provide opportunities for commercial, cultural, and political contacts.

All ambassadors based in Washington must decide how much time, attention, and energy they should devote to travel outside Washington. Some decide to make travel a very high priority. For example, a former Austrian ambassador to Washington, Helmut Tuerk, made it a point to visit all fifty states. If there was something of a gimmick aspect to touching toes in all American states, there was also a strategy at work. In his travels, Tuerk contacted state and local officials, and these contacts often gave him an entrée to leading members of Congress and the administration. For example, a meeting with the governor or secretary of state of Oregon would often give him the opening to call on members of the state's congressional delegation to pass on greetings and suggest lunch.

Despite the lure of the road, Eliasson decided early in his tenure that he would limit his travel within the United States. He averaged about four or five trips a year. Traveling, he says, is fun, invigorating, and provided him with a helpful perspective on how the rest of the country saw Washington and the world. And there were opportunities to meet leaders in business and government and the Swedish American community.

Working closely with his assistant, Monica Lundkvist, and Sweden's far-flung network of honorary consuls, Eliasson arranged his trips so he touched a number of bases. For example, when he hit the road he scheduled meetings with state and local government officials, gave speeches to local chambers of commerce, presented lectures at colleges and universities, and attended receptions held by Swedish American groups.

Making quick mental calculations, Eliasson told me that during his time as ambassador he made five trips to Minnesota; five to Illinois; three to California; two to Washington state, Michigan, and Texas; and single visits to Arizona, (where he was given a personal tour by Justice O'Connor) Kansas, Louisiana, North Carolina, and Iowa. He said he took frequent trips to New York and four or five to Boston.

The ambassador says these trips offered him a fresh perspective and a renewed sense of the scope and diversity of the United States. And often they gave him a jolt of adrenaline.

"If I'm ever lacking in self-confidence I go to Minnesota," he says. But he adds that travel takes time, is often very tiring, and pulled him away from his main job: connecting with Washington policy makers.

"I've been all over. It's always fun and interesting to get another perspective. And I wish I had more time to do it," he said. "But it takes a toll. I come back tired. A lot of the travel seems to be over the weekend. And when I return there is so much to do in Washington. I feel Washington should be given the highest priority. There is so much going on here—things only an ambassador can do."

CHAPTER 12

Prestigious Prizes

Jan and Kerstin Eliasson at the embassy's Nobel Prize dinner with Energy Secretary
Samuel Bodman

&a I &a

If there was a signature moment of Jan Eliasson's tenure in Washington, it
was probably in late November 2001 at the White House when he took
part in a ceremony commemorating the one hundredth anniversary of the
Nobel Prize.

President Bush presided over the ceremony for thirty-seven past American winners of the Nobel Prize and six of the eight American winners of the 2001 prizes.

"Each Nobel laureate here today belongs to an incredibly select group of people," Bush said before the invited guests in the East Room of the White House. "It includes the names of Martin Luther King Jr., George C. Marshall, T. S. Eliot, Albert Einstein, Vice President Charles Dawes, and President Theodore Roosevelt—the first American Nobel laureate, whose Peace Prize today occupies a place of honor in the West Wing of the White House.

"Many awards recognize excellence. The Nobel Foundation recognizes greatness," Bush said, adding that "the annual selection of the laureates expresses a profound optimism about humanity and our prospects for improvement."

Eliasson followed Bush to the podium and emphasized how important the Nobel prizes have been to Sweden over the past century. After Bush and the ambassador spoke, Jan and Kerstin Eliasson were asked by Condoleezza Rice to join George and Laura Bush at the head of the receiving line.

"This made some of my colleagues in the diplomatic corps feel a tinge of envy," Eliasson recalled. He said the receiving line took on a comic air when Henry Kissinger, the winner of the 1973 peace prize, met him in line. Sweden had been a fierce critic of the Vietnam war, and Kissinger had offered scathing public criticisms of Sweden. Eliasson was a senior diplomat in Sweden's Washington embassy during that time.

In Eliasson's account of the encounter with Kissinger, offered with a credible imitation of Kissinger's voice, the former secretary of state was surprised and amused to be greeted by Eliasson. "Mr. Ambassador, I would not have expected to be greeted at the White House by the Swedish ambassador," Kissinger told Eliasson.

෯ II ෯

In his attempts to put Sweden on the Washington map, Jan Eliasson had to use creativity, cunning, and persistence. But he was also given one advantage that he came to regard as valuable as gold: the Nobel prizes. Eliasson viewed the Nobel prizes as both a message and an opportunity. The message is that Sweden, the home of the world's most prestigious awards, is an important nation in which excellence and even greatness are celebrated.

The opportunity Eliasson seized was to use the annual awarding of the Nobel prizes as a way to refresh and expand high-level contacts with the White

House and the broader political community in Washington and the scientific community in the United States.

"The word 'Nobel' is better known than 'Sweden' in the United States. Nobel has meant a tremendous amount to us—not only as a symbol of science and research and the pursuit of knowledge. But it's a fantastic way to develop contacts in the university world and also the political world in Washington," Eliasson said.

The Nobel Prize is an international award given every year since 1901 for achievements in physics, chemistry, medicine, literature, and peace. In 1968, the Bank of Sweden created a prize for economics. The prizewinners, who are announced in October each year, receive their awards (a monetary award, a gold medal, and a diploma) on December 10 in Stockholm, the anniversary of Alfred Nobel's death. The awards are officially conferred at a glittering event in Stockholm's City Hall, which the king and queen of Sweden attend. The Peace Prize is given in Oslo, Norway.

Alfred Nobel was born in 1833 in Stockholm. A scientist, inventor, and businessman, Nobel invented dynamite in 1866 and later built companies and laboratories in more than twenty nations around the world. On November 27, 1895, Nobel signed his last will providing for the establishment of the Nobel Prize. He died in his home in Italy on December 10, 1896.

Since the award's inception, more than a third of the winners have been Americans. Seizing on this fact, Swedish ambassadors in Washington have held receptions and dinners in connection to the prize. Eliasson accepted this tradition and expanded it. During his tenure, he used the annual awarding of Nobel prizes to host three events: a press briefing at a hotel near the embassy so journalists could interview the American laureates, a reception at the White House, and a black-tie dinner at his residence.

The press briefing was an innovation by Eliasson with his wife and has been a good technique to increase the prize's Washington visibility. The Swedish embassy invites several dozen journalists to attend a briefing at a hotel in downtown Washington. Eliasson gives introductory remarks about the Nobel Prize and introduces each of the American laureates who would then go to a small round table and speak with reporters about their research and careers.

The Eliassons quickly recognized that the reception held at the White House for the laureates and special guests was something they needed to protect at all costs. The annual Nobel receptions at the White House, the ambassador said, "gave us a fantastic opportunity to meet the president, the first lady, and members of the cabinet every year."

Eliasson said that in two of the years that he was in Washington the White House reception was nearly canceled. In both cases, Eliasson swung into high gear to get the reception placed back on the schedule. This involved an intense, governmentwide lobbying campaign in which the ambassador personally called his midlevel and higher contacts at the State Department and the NSC, the State Department's Office of Protocol, the first lady's office, contacts in the U.S. science community, and anyone else who might have the president's ear.

"When the reception was almost canceled one year, Eliasson pushed about as aggressively as you can in diplomacy to get it back on the calendar," recalled Heather Conley. "He worked all of his contacts. He was utterly determined," she said.

Eliasson recognized that if the event is canceled once, it could easily be dropped from the schedule altogether. "This reception is so important for Sweden. We can't lose it," Eliasson said. "I told my successor he should do everything to keep this event going. Everything," Eliasson added.

The black-tie dinner at the ambassador's residence is a highly coveted invitation in Washington. Typically, the residence accommodates about forty guests for a sit-down dinner, but the ambassador's staff would rearrange the dining room so eighty guests could be accommodated. Eliasson used the allure of an elegant dinner with Nobel laureates to invite Supreme Court justices, cabinet secretaries, senior congressmen, and think tank leaders to his home. And he savored the cumulative candlepower he assembled.

"We have the highest concentration of brainpower in the metropolitan area, or I would go further and say the United States, here tonight," he said as he welcomed laureates from the 1950s through 2001.

During the dinner in 2001, Chief Justice William Rehnquist thanked Eliasson for the opportunity to mingle with such intellectual luminaries, adding that he hoped he would "get smarter." "After several years, it certainly has not happened to me," Rehnquist joked.

Trying to keep the evening interesting and even a little playful, the ambassador and his wife fielded questions from the guests to direct to the laureates. Some were serious; others jocular. Eliasson once forwarded a question if the scientists would choose a Nobel Prize over their wives. Or how similar a worm is to a human being and should the similarity be of concern? Or if telescopic X-ray astronomy could help us communicate with extraterrestrials?

Eliasson said the Nobel dinner has been critical for Sweden's visibility in Washington. "For me, it's crucial that our visibility be maintained. We should be seen as an actor in this city. The Nobel Prize has been one of our greatest

Jan and Kerstin Eliasson speak to Rice at a reception for Nobel Prize winners

assets in making Sweden known to the world. Each year, this is one of the few times that Sweden makes the front pages of the world's newspapers," he said.

ૐ III ૐ

On a chilly March night in Washington, Eliasson presided over a small reception at his residence where Strobe Talbott, the former deputy secretary of state and now the president of the Brookings Institution, was awarded Sweden's Royal Order of Polar Star. While obviously not as prestigious as the Nobel, the Polar Star is an award Sweden gives to recognize and thank people from other countries who have been helpful to Sweden.

On this night about thirty guests have gathered at the Eliasson's residence for the reception for Talbott. The guest list includes the ambassadors from the United Kingdom; Finland; and Estonia; and the president of the World Bank, Jim Wolfensohn, and his wife, Elaine. Eliasson is relaxed and informal, sipping wine, munching on Swedish hors d'oeuvres, and chatting with Talbott and his wife, Brooke.

After about forty-five minutes, Eliasson ushers Talbott to a corner of the room. The two stand under a glittering chandelier, next to a grand piano. Eliasson tells the assembled guests that Talbott was named a commander of the Royal Order of the Polar Star for his contributions to cooperation and security in the region around the Baltic Sea. The ambassador says that during his time at the State Department Talbott worked with Sweden and other Nordic nations to integrate Estonia, Lithuania, and Latvia into the Baltic and Transatlantic communities.

This, Eliasson believes, was one of the most important diplomatic accomplishments of his professional lifetime. And he credits Talbott for being an important contributor to this success story. The Baltic Sea area, Eliasson said, is "an area of good news in a world of bad news."

Speaking warmly, he recalls his work with Talbott when both served as deputy foreign ministers. He says that Talbott's constructive efforts in the Baltic region are greatly appreciated in Sweden.

"It's the most important change that has affected our nation, this evolution-ary and revolutionary change in the Baltic Sea region. It has changed the map for us. It has brought about a modern Hanseatic league around the Baltic Sea. We were an outpost of democracy during the Cold War," the ambassador says.

Eliasson gives a brief history of the award before placing the Polar Star around Talbott's neck. He says that Sweden's Royal Order of Polar Star is awarded by the king of Sweden in consultation with the government. It was started by King Fredrik I in 1748 and is given to people of great merit in the civil sphere, the sciences, literature, industry, and trade. Since 1975, the Polar Star has been awarded only to foreign nationals to recognize their personal services to Sweden or for the promotion of Swedish interests.

The badge consists of a white Maltese cross set in gold with open gold crowns in the angles between the arms of the cross. The blue medallion in the center contains a white polar star with the legend Nescit Occasum (It never sets). The badge is surmounted by a gold royal crown and is attached to a blue silk ribbon with gold edges.

After the ambassador placed the Polar Star on Talbott, the recipient acknowledged his father and wife, thanked Eliasson for his warm words, and said how impressed he has been with Eliasson as a diplomat.

৯৯ IV ৯৯

While other Swedish embassies also confer the Polar Star, several Swedish diplomats said that Eliasson approached the award with a strategic perspective. The ambassador said he viewed the award as an instrument of diplomacy.

"I take it up at a staff meeting and say this is the time to start thinking of the decoration. I tell them to remember that this is a very important tool to confirm and thank people for what they've done. It gives tremendous goodwill. It has links to Swedish history. It's one of the oldest decorations in the world. The goodwill we get from it is very high. It's a nice thing. It adds to the personal element of diplomacy. I go through it every year rather carefully."

CHAPTER 13

Breaking into the News

Eliasson listens as a Swedish reporter questions Colin Powell

۶ـؤ **I** ۶ـؤ

Throughout his diplomatic career, Jan Eliasson has liked the press, has liked being in the press, and has liked Sweden being mentioned in the press. If the ambassador's relationship with the press was not precisely a full-scale love affair, it was a strategic, purposeful, and assiduous flirtation.

"I like dealing with the press. There have been no disasters yet," he said, shortly before leaving Washington and after a nearly forty-year career in diplomacy. The ambassador's supporters say his direct approach to the media is a welcome dose of transparency and openness in a profession that is not distinguished by transparency or openness. His critics say that there's been more than a touch of self-promotion involved in Eliasson's press outreach.

During his time in Washington, Eliasson read newspapers, watched television news, took careful note of who was being mentioned, and circulated articles to his staff containing his scrawled notes and underlines. He enjoyed being mentioned. Getting noticed by Washington's press corps was not Eliasson's central priority, but it was a secondary goal that related to his determination that Sweden be seen and heard in Washington.

Viewed by reporters as intelligent, experienced, and fun, Eliasson popped up in the Washington press with some frequency, especially given that Sweden was rarely front-page news in the United States. He frequently came across reporters in his public work, especially when he attended think tank events, receptions, and conferences. His approach was a respectful, mostly low-key cultivation. He invited journalists to embassy receptions and kept in touch with them. During social events, Eliasson would drop quips, tips, and observations that sometimes made it into the newspapers and then into the broader political discussion in Washington.

֍ II ֍

For most ambassadors, Washington's press corps is a large, multilayered, complicated behemoth that does not seem very interested in what diplomats do on a regular basis. On those occasions when an ambassador's country is in the news, there is often a spike of interest, but this almost always fades as quickly as it arises. The simple fact is that few journalists or news organizations follow Washington's diplomatic community on a day-to-day basis. Large newspapers such as the *Washington Post, New York Times,* and *Wall Street Journal* have diplomatic correspondents, but they mostly cover the State Department, Pentagon, and American intelligence agencies. Similarly, diplomatic correspondents for major TV networks typically don't cover diplomats on a regular basis.

Several specialty publications, such as the *Washington Diplomat* and *Diplomatic Traffic,* cover the diplomatic corps. And party or society reporters for the *Washington Post* and *Washington Times* write stories about diplomats that are read by the public and policy makers.

While the post–September 11 climate in Washington was far more open to international affairs than before, this interest tended to be issue-specific with a focus on terrorism or intelligence reform, or country-specific with attention paid to developments in Pakistan or China or Saudi Arabia. In fact, at the end of 2002, the one outlet that was specifically interested in the work of diplomats, Washington's venerable Overseas Writers Organization, scaled back its operations after more than eighty years. The demise of the club was attributed to the rise of cable television outlets that journalists used to cover the news by watching them rather than cultivating sources.

The ambassador brought both a message and a strategy to his dealings with the Washington press corps. His message was that Sweden was an active, responsible, vibrant country that was a committed member of the European Union and a regional leader in northern Europe. Eliasson discussed issues important to Sweden, such as the importance of the United Nations and the growing problem of trafficking in persons. He also presented himself as a European diplomat who could offer that perspective to the Washington policy debate.

His strategy was to reach out widely to the members of the press corps who may be inclined—or persuaded—to write about Sweden and his work in Washington. He focused sharply on the two major newspapers in the city: the *Washington Post* and the *Washington Times*. The ambassador got to know and even cultivated a number of *Washington Post* reporters who write about international affairs and diplomacy, such as Walter Pincus, Jim Hoagland, Fred Hiatt, and Jackson Diehl. He kept in close contact with Nora Boustany, who writes the *Post's* twice-a-week "Diplomatic Dispatches" column. Eliasson closely followed her column, which largely chronicles the activity of foreign diplomats in Washington.

The ambassador also made contacts at the rival paper, the *Washington Times*. Two of its reporters who cover Washington's diplomatic community, James Morrison and Kevin Chafee, were frequents guests at Swedish embassy receptions. Morrison writes the *Washington Times* "Embassy Row" column.

"Republicans read the *Washington Times*," he said.

Media luminaries attended receptions at Eliasson's residence over the years: Ben Bradlee and Sally Quinn of the *Washington Post*, Jim Lehrer Margaret Warner and Ray Suarez from the *NewsHour with Jim Lehrer*, Chris Matthews from MSNBC, and Lally Weymouth from *Newsweek*.

On two occasions, Weymouth invited Eliasson to be one of *Newsweek's* guests at the White House Correspondents' Dinner. The *Newsweek* table is one of the most prestigious tables. Eliasson said those dinners were a "good chance to present Sweden" to Washington, but he acknowledged it was also very good for people watching.

"I met the most incredible collection of people. There were only four or five other ambassadors there. It's not easy to get in," he told me after one dinner. He was also invited to the prestigious Gridiron Dinner by Georgie Ann Geyer, an international affairs columnist.

The ambassador also met about every six weeks with a small group of Swedish reporters based in Washington. Journalists who met with Eliasson represented Sweden's two leading newspapers, *Dagens Nyheter* and *Svenska Dagbladet*, as well as the Swedish Television Company and Swedish Radio. The sessions were mostly informal conversations over coffee.

"I think I had a very warm relationship with the Swedish press corps in Washington, but it wasn't that operational. My primary job was to develop contacts with the American press," the ambassador says.

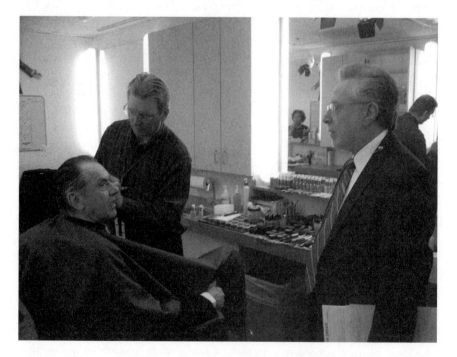

Eliasson prepares to appear on CNN with Wolf Blitzer

❧ III ❧

During his five years in Washington, from September 1, 2000, to July 1, 2005, Eliasson was mentioned in thirty stories in the *Washington Post* and thirty-nine stories in the *Washington Times*.

By comparison, two respected ambassadors from countries of a similar stature in Washington, Chan Heng Chee from Singapore and Michael Thawley of Australia, appeared much less often. Ambassador Chan was mentioned in thirteen stories in the *Washington Times* and *Washington Post* during this same period, while Thawley was mentioned in twenty-three stories. Interestingly, at the time both Singapore and Australia had major trade agreements with the United States pending in Congress, so their ambassadors may have had more reason to be in the news.

During this same five-year period, Prince Bandar, Saudi Arabia's ambassador and the city's most public diplomatic figure, was mentioned in two hundred and forty stories.

In the Post, the first and last articles about Eliasson were wide-ranging and extensive profiles. But most of the mentions of him were sightings at parties or comments at various occasions such as the embassy's Lucia party and the Nobel dinners. Several of the articles related to Sweden's decision to build a new embassy in Washington. Several also pertained to the tragic killing of Sweden's foreign minister, Anna Lindh, in September of 2003.

Usually skillful with a quote, Eliasson described one concert performed by the Swedish Radio Symphony Orchestra with the Swedish Radio Choir and the Eric Ericsson Chamber Choir as a "rendezvous with angels." And he called a Swedish design exhibit that opened in Washington shortly after September 11 as "a tribute to normalcy, to sanity, to daily life . . . a little pearl in the middle of Washington in these sad times."

Eliasson made substantive comments about policy in only a handful of the articles. He voiced some frustration with Washington's media game. "It's hard to get anything in the *Post*," he said.

The ambassador appeared on several significant television programs. He was on the *NewsHour with Jim Lehrer* during the run-up to the Iraq war in the winter of 2003 to offer an assessment of his fellow Swede Hans Blix, the chief of the UN Monitoring, Verification, and Inspection Commission. Eliasson described Blix as "a very skilled international lawyer" who could be relied on to submit a "factual and correct report." Speaking in full diplomatic mode, Eliasson said that he believed all parties "including the president of the United States," preferred a peaceful resolution of the Iraq conflict.

Several years later, Eliasson appeared on CNN and Fox to discuss the devastating consequences of the 2004 tsunami on hundreds of Swedes who were traveling in southeast Asia. Eliasson participated in a number of foreign policy panels, several related to the United Nations, that were covered on C-SPAN. This gave him a national audience to articulate his views.

In the fall of 2004 the ambassador and his wife were the subject of a major profile in *Washington Life* magazine with a number of photographs. The article likened him to James Bond because of his "charm, elegance and rugged good looks." The James Bond analogy caught on and was referred to in other articles. Congressman Tom Lantos even mentioned it during a speech on the floor of the House of Representatives in May 2005 in which he paid tribute to Eliasson's diplomacy in Washington.

Just after his tenure in Washington ended and Eliasson had moved to New York to become president of the UN General Assembly, the ambassador was the subject of extensive profiles in the *New York Times* and in *Nordic Reach* magazine that included several photographs of him with Colin Powell.

Eliasson appearing on CNN

Eliasson did not use the embassy's Web site to outline his views or provide access to his speeches and writings. The Swedish embassy sent out occasional press releases, but did not publish a regular newsletter as do other middle-sized embassies such as Singapore and Australia.

⳥ IV ⳥

While the ambassador was sometimes teased by colleagues and his staff for enjoying the media spotlight, Eliasson was aggressive in looking for ways to get other Swedes mentioned in the Washington press. When Foreign Minister Freivalds visited Washington in February 2004, Eliasson hosted a reception for her at his residence. As the evening was winding down and Freivalds was beginning to relax with a small group of guests in the ambassador's library, Eliasson noticed that Boustany, the *Post's* diplomatic reporter, had just arrived. Determined to arrange a one-on-one interview between Freivalds and Boustany, Eliasson, in a polite but firm way, escorted everyone else out of his library. A private interview took place and several days later Freivalds was featured in Boustany's column, describing her background and views on foreign policy.

CHAPTER 14

The European

Eliasson with Representative Tom Lantos, senior Democrat on the House International Relations Committee

৪৯ I ৪৯

Within Sweden's diplomatic community, Jan Eliasson is regarded as an expert on the United States and the United Nations. Some in Stockholm have faulted him for being insufficiently focused on, or interested in, the European Union, especially its bureaucratic machinery.

It's somewhat ironic that it was during Eliasson's time as ambassador in Washington that he says he first fully felt his identity as a European. Sweden held the rotating EU presidency from January through June 2001. This propelled Eliasson into the role as one of the EU's chief spokesmen and representatives in Washington. Eliasson says his European identify came alive in Washington as he grew more convinced that only a strong, unified Europe would have sufficient stature and strength to be taken seriously in the world and in the United States.

The ambassador also believes a stronger Europe is good for the prosperity and security of its citizens and that a stronger European relationship with the United States is beneficial for the world, helping to prevent and solve problems.

❧ II ❧

Eliasson arrived in Washington in the early fall of 2000 as the Clinton administration was winding down and a fiercely contested presidential race was heating up. Europe and the United States disagreed on a number of issues during the Clinton years, including the most appropriate policy for the war-torn Balkans. But the transatlantic relationship was solid and mostly positive. Clinton spoke a language and employed a diplomatic style that Europeans generally liked and appreciated. Clinton was careful to consult Europeans on most issues. In fact, this penchant to consult was one of the arguments Texas Governor George W. Bush used against the Clinton-Gore administration. He felt their consultation edged toward deference.

The Bush administration's assumption to power in 2001 was a jolt for many Europeans. While Bush spoke in conciliatory tones during the campaign about the need for a humble American foreign policy, the first months of the new administration signaled that there would be a different kind of transatlantic relationship. In words and action, the Bush administration indicated it would approach the world far differently than the Clinton administration. In its early months, the administration opposed the Comprehensive Test Ban Treaty, derailed a conference on slowing the proliferation of small arms and light weapons, proclaimed the Kyoto Protocol on global warming as dead, and trashed the International Criminal Court. Bush also vowed to withdraw from the Anti-Ballistic Missile Treaty and to proceed with a national missile defense program, a move that many Europeans saw as provocative and potentially destabilizing.

Coupled with these hard-line views was a diplomatic style that was harsh and often dismissive of differing opinions. Eliasson sensed early in 2001 that the Bush administration's approach to specific issues and its views on diplomacy would not be well received in Sweden or elsewhere in Europe.

"We had a sense this was not going so well. We had a public row over Kyoto. It was followed by other issues: the International Criminal Court, the Comprehensive Test Ban Treaty. There was a growing discomfort on the European side," he recalled.

Against this emerging backdrop Sweden assumed the EU's six-month rotating presidency in January 2001, just as a new administration was coming to power. As president, Sweden organized the EU's work program for the first half of 2001 and served as its public face.

Eliasson hosted a lunch at his embassy with EU ambassadors in Washington and the new National Security Council, Advisor Condoleezza Rice. Eliasson said the session was an important opportunity for him to get to know Rice and her team at the NSC as well as European experts at the State Department.

"It put Sweden on the map to an extraordinary degree. This was a tremendous introduction to political life in Washington. I met people at the highest level. I used those personal contacts for the rest of my time in Washington," he said. "We were given a strong platform in the transatlantic dialogue when we held the presidency of the EU. We came into contact with Colin Powell and Condi Rice and their closest advisors on the transatlantic relationship."

Eliasson consulted closely with the Bush administration and EU officials in Brussels in the spring of 2001 when a war looked likely in Macedonia. But working together, the United States and European Union were able to help defuse the crisis. This confirmed for Eliasson that when Americans and Europeans worked cooperatively, good things could happen.

"I think the combined muscle power of the U.S. and EU was very important in preventing another war from breaking out in Macedonia. The pride I felt as a European, working hand in hand with the U.S, is something I treasure very much," he said.

In addition to giving him a crash course on the practical aspects of EU programs and institutions, Eliasson's responsibility to represent both Sweden and the European Union in Washington gave him a new sense of European identity.

"It was during this time that I for the first time really felt as a strong European," he said.

✌ III ✌

On September 11, 2001, Eliasson was in his limousine approaching the Swedish embassy in downtown Washington when he received a call on his cell phone from his sister-in-law in Sweden asking about the attacks and making sure he was OK. Eliasson hustled upstairs to the office, watched events unfold on TV, allowed staffers to leave who felt they needed to go home, and spent the rest of the day monitoring events and getting in touch with the State Department's number three diplomat, Marc Grossman.

Eliasson said he understood very quickly that 9/11 would change American foreign policy and possibly recast its relationship with Europe.

"In one of my first reports after 9/11 I said I think this will change the course of history, change the course of American foreign policy. One of my colleagues thought I highly exaggerated. When I saw him last year he said I was closer to being right," Eliasson said.

While all of Europe strongly supported the United States after 9/11, tensions mounted when the Bush administration shifted its attention to Iraq and developed the strategy of preemption that deeply troubled many in Europe and Sweden. Sweden's view was that any attempt to launch a war to remove Saddam Hussein required approval by the UN Security Council.

"Europe was very strongly divided. We couldn't speak with one voice. It was a low point to represent Europe in Washington," he recalls, adding that these differences were noticed by the administration and even exacerbated by its references to Old and New Europe.

"Sweden took a mid position, questioning the legitimacy of the operation and the wisdom of the operation. Sweden is a country that is strongly attached to international law," the ambassador said. But Eliasson counseled other Europeans in Washington to tone down the sharp rhetoric directed toward the United States.

"I know what Saddam's regime was like. In Sweden we were strongly in favor of not hurting the dialogue between the United States and Europe," he said. "The American side appreciated that we are strong voices for transatlantic relations."

After the Iraq war was launched in early 2003, Eliasson urged Europeans to focus on finding common projects that would bring the transatlantic alliance back together. These projects include waging a fight against terrorism in the context of international law, controlling the proliferation of weapons of mass destruction, promoting peace and stability in the Middle East, and supporting democracy and free markets.

Eliasson chats with Norway's ambassador to the U.S, Knut Vollebaek

"The White House's language about democracy is a little dramatic, a bit of rhetoric, but it's our values. It's our program as well," he said.

❧ IV ❧

During his time in Washington, Eliasson was part of several different European communities. As one of twenty-five ambassadors from the European Union, Eliasson worked with the European Commission's delegation in Washington. The commission is the executive branch of the European Union and has maintained an office and an ambassador in Washington for many years.

Eliasson attended the monthly meetings of EU ambassadors, although he was not reluctant to duck out if he felt the sessions were not productive. Never a fan of large meetings, Eliasson felt it made more sense for EU ambassadors to meet in smaller groups and do substantive diplomatic work. He consulted closely with the other Nordic and Baltic ambassadors in Washington, for instance, seeing this as an important community that

Sweden has plausible and historic leadership claims to. A member of the European Union only since 1995 and one of its smaller countries in terms of population, Sweden is not a natural leader of the larger European Union. But it is a natural leader of the Baltic world.

"The Nordic-Baltic relationship has grown. Sweden is a country of some significance in the Baltic area. We are the biggest of the Baltic-Nordic nations. Globally, Sweden doesn't have much of an impact. But we can have an impact in our neighborhood," the ambassador said.

Eliasson worked closely with the State Department in crafting the e-Pine program, sensing that a new project was needed to keep the United States connected to northern Europe.

"The ambassador understood far better than most that it was important to find a new project to keep the United States interested in northern Europe. He grasped that immediately," said former State Department diplomat Heather Conley.

Eliasson, like other European ambassadors, relished the opportunity to be a spokesman for Europe and to offer a European perspective to the United States' political debates.

"There needs to be a European voice in these debates. We've tried to be a sensible European voice," he said.

But he also liked to highlight Sweden as a unique country with its own special traditions and insights. He worked cooperatively with other European ambassadors in Washington, but there was a quiet competition to get the ear and respect of American leaders. By the end of his time in Washington, Eliasson said the American-European relationship had substantially improved, with a more positive tone and with important projects under way in the Middle East, the Balkans, Afghanistan, and elsewhere.

Richard Solomon, president of the U.S. Institute of Peace, credits Eliasson for working to defuse anti-American sentiment that was building across Europe.

"Eliasson was deeply worried about the anti-Americanism in Europe. I think he played some role in intra-European discussions trying to convince Europeans that this anti-Americanism was not good for them," Solomon said. "Eliasson believed that the U.S. is playing an active and leading role in world affairs. He was personally disturbed by anti-American feeling in European affairs. I would be very surprised if Eliasson wasn't given a pretty good hearing by the administration. He was one of the real critics of the anti-Americanism in Europe. He was a real asset in Washington."

CHAPTER 15

The Boss

Eliasson meets with his staff in his office

❧ I ❧

Twice a week Jan Eliasson assembled his staff in a modest-sized conference room in Sweden's downtown embassy for a meeting that was known as "morning prayer." About two dozen diplomats would sit around a large, circular, wooden table with twenty-five miniature flags of the EU nations in the middle. Support staff typically sat in chairs against the wall.

Eliasson would often begin with light banter about the weekend or offer an anecdote or story. He once cracked up the meeting by describing how he locked himself out of his residence compound and had to climb over a large fence to get in—as one of his neighbors peered out the window, looking on in bemused amazement.

But he quickly got to business. Eliasson would summarize the main projects he was working on, recount pertinent conversations with American officials, discuss any news he had from Stockholm, and then go around the table asking staffers to briefly discuss what they were working on and what issues should be brought to his attention. Attentive and intense, Eliasson would jot down notes, ask questions, offer comments, or nod his head in agreement. At the end of the forty-five-minute session, Eliasson would ask a few staffers to remain behind so he could follow up on items that were either too technical or too sensitive for the large group meeting. He also held smaller meetings once a month for about a dozen of his most senior diplomats.

The ambassador's management style was to praise people in public and reserve any criticisms or reservations for private sessions. He did not bark out orders or push people hard in large settings. Eliasson was by most accounts a pleasant, purposeful, good-humored, and demanding boss. When he got interested in a topic, he plowed in and became immersed in details. His search for more information sometimes had a scattershot, even haphazard quality. Staffers sometimes grumbled that more than one person was working on the same project.

Affable and approachable, Eliasson was well liked by his staff. They called him by his first name and could even gently tease him about his frequent notes and penchant for micromanagement. No one seemed intimidated by Eliasson, but it was always clear who was in charge of the embassy.

Throughout his career, Eliasson has been lavishly praised for his communication skills, political insights, networking abilities, and diplomatic shrewdness. But he's been praised less for his interest in routine administration and budgeting.

ᵺᴁ II ᵺᴁ

Modern ambassadors should be viewed less as conduits of private information between leaders at home and the host government and more as executives who oversee the national account of a multinational firm.

They are the official representatives of their government to the host government and have the cachet of an impressive title and diplomatic privileges. But they are also involved in more prosaic work like managing a staff, establishing a coherent work program, and selling an image of their home to the host country.

In Eliasson's case, he managed Sweden's American account. The United States is the most important country in the world for Sweden and Eliasson's job was to monitor this relationship and prevent strains from developing, if possible.

More prosaically, he was also the boss of about forty-five employees at the Swedish embassy, a mix of professional diplomats and local hires. The Washington embassy is one of Sweden's largest, but it's a relatively small embassy by Washington standards. The British, Russian, Chinese, Japanese, and Canadian embassies in Washington have hundreds of diplomats and support staff. The American embassy in Bogota employs nearly one thousand people.

When you walk the halls of the Swedish embassy in Washington, the prevalent mood is of purposeful but subdued efficiency. People are serious and professional, but unhurried. There is no frantic racing down the halls that you see on the *West Wing* TV show or even the steady buzz you see in the halls of Congress. Swedish diplomats arrive early and leave, for the most part, early. The workday officially ends at 5 p.m. Very few people are still around after six in the evening.

The embassy's ambience is neat and orderly; tasteful, modern Swedish art and large coffee-table books from Sweden are scattered about. The wall colors are soft and gentle and soothing. Office doors are left open, except when people are attending meetings or have left for the day. People gather to have coffee and chat in the late morning in a conference room next to the small kitchen.

As a community of Swedes away from home, Sweden's embassy staff holds parties and socializes together, while also attempting to integrate into Washington life.

৯৯ III ৯৯

The two focal points of Eliasson's Washington life were his residence in northwest Washington and the embassy in downtown Washington. The residence's upstairs apartments for the ambassador and his family include a small kitchen, a study, a living room, and a bedroom. There is also a guest suite for important visitors such as the prime minister or the king and queen. The residence's elegant first-floor reception rooms are used for parties, dinners, and working lunches.

During Eliasson's ambassadorship, the Swedish embassy was located in downtown Washington, at the intersection of 15th and M streets. The embassy occupied the ninth and tenth floors of a modern office building, across the street from the Madison Hotel.

Eliasson presided over a staff of about fifty, organized into nine sections. Of this group, twenty-nine were Stockholm-based diplomats and nineteen were local hires. Fourteen were from the Foreign Ministry, five were from the Defense Ministry, four from the Science Ministry, and there was one each from the Culture, Finance, and Industry ministries. There was also a staffer from the Swedish Trade Council.

As the ambassador, Eliasson served as an active CEO who oversaw the embassy's main projects and programs. The deputy chief of mission (DCM) served as a chief operating officer who was responsible for making sure operations ran smoothly. During Eliasson's tenure, he had two DCMs: Bo Eriksson and Caroline Vicini.

Each of the nine sections of the embassy is headed up by a counselor or a minister. The Political Affairs section handles bilateral political issues and reports on trends in American foreign policy. The Trade and Economic Affairs unit monitors American trade policy and helps the Swedish government and businesses make contacts with American leaders. It serves as a link between Sweden and the World Bank and the Inter-American Development Bank. The Press, Culture, and Information section monitors the American press and keeps in contact with Swedish journalists posted in the United States. The cultural unit tries to present a positive image of Swedish culture through exhibits and visiting artists and reports back to Sweden about American cultural trends.

The Consular and Administrative Affairs section is run by a counselor, Pomtus Jarborg, who is head of the chancery, the embassy's office, and is in charge of personnel matters, daily administration and housing. The Finance and Economic Affairs section follows and reports back to Sweden about economic and financial developments in the United States. It passes on information about the Swedish economy to interested parties in the States. The Labor and Social Affairs unit disseminates information about Sweden's labor market and monitors the American labor market. The Swedish Trade Council operates from the embassy and includes several people working on defense industry programs.

The ambassador relaxes with his press counselor, Claes Thorson, in Gotland, Sweden

The Science and Technology unit monitors and develops contacts within the American scientific community. Kerstin Eliasson ran this unit until she accepted a job in Stockholm in early 2004 to serve as the deputy minister for education. The Defense section works in a secure corridor of the embassy that requires a special code to enter. It provides information about Sweden's defense programs and industry, linking Sweden and American defense establishments.

Additionally, Sweden has a consul general in New York and Los Angeles and will open one in Houston in 2007. It has four honorary consuls general, based in San Francisco, Minneapolis, Chicago, and Detroit. There is also a network of more than thirty honorary consulates. These are typically headed up by prominent Americans with Swedish ancestry who run these honorary consulates out of their homes or businesses.

ॐ IV ॐ

If the center of American diplomacy is the drab State Department building in the Foggy Bottom neighborhood in Washington, the epicenter of Swedish diplomacy is the Arvfurstens Palace in Stockholm, a French-country-manor-style palace that was built for Princess Sofia Albertina in 1794. It's now the home of the Swedish Foreign Ministry. Opposite the Royal Opera House and with clear views of the Royal Palace and the Parliament, the palace has been the center of Swedish diplomacy for a century.

Sweden has a significant diplomatic apparatus. It has one hundred and two overseas missions, which include embassies, representations, delegations, and consulates. Sweden has eighty-four embassies; the largest are in Washington, London, Brussels, Berlin, Moscow, and Beijing. The size of Sweden's missions range from one to about fifty. Smaller missions have two or three staff, while the larger ones have fifteen or more. Most of the missions abroad have between three and six diplomats.

Sweden has seven delegations and representations to such organizations as the European Union, the United Nations, and the Organization of Economic Cooperation and Development in Paris. These missions are set up to monitor, represent, and promote all aspects of Swedish interests in the country of their operations or in international organizations such as the United Nations. They are also responsible for providing services to Swedish agencies, companies, organizations, and individual citizens. A priority task of missions is to promote economic interests abroad by providing services to Swedish companies and encouraging foreign investment in Sweden.

Disseminating information about Sweden is also an important responsibility for all the country's embassies. Sweden's Foreign Ministry employs about 2,450 people. About 900 are based in Stockholm, while the rest work abroad. Typically, an overseas posting for a Swedish diplomat means working consecutively at two missions for a total of seven to ten years. Then a four- to six-year period at home is expected. When working abroad, diplomats receive a tax-free supplement for additional costs in addition to their salaries that are taxed in Sweden.

If American diplomacy continues to be dominated by men, there is a distinctly feminine cast to Swedish diplomacy. Nearly 60 percent of Sweden's Foreign Ministry staff are women. The average age is forty-six and more than half have been employed by the Foreign Ministry for more than ten years. The top tier of the Foreign Ministry is headed up by the foreign minister, the deputy foreign minister, the minister for migration and asylum, and the minister for international development.

The work of the Washington embassy is overseen by the Americas Department within the Foreign Ministry. The Americas Department comprises fifteen diplomats who are responsible for Sweden's foreign trade and

Eliasson confers with Lennart Johansson, Sweden's Consul General in Detroit and Lisa Svensson, an embassy staffer

development cooperation policy relations with the nations of North America, Central America, South America, and the Caribbean.

ಜಿ V ಜಿ

Eliasson believed that while his job had administrative and management responsibilities, these should not be the focus of his work. He delegated much of the routine administration to his DCM and the director of consular and administrative affairs and focused on his political work.

"It's generally recognized at a top embassy the ambassador should be free to do the political work and the external work while the number two is the one to keep track of the internal things. This is a classic division of labor, which I don't mind in this case. But if it wasn't working I think I would do something," he said. "I don't think administration is the best way to spend my time. My comparative advantage is persuasion and people contacts, building high-level contacts and writing analysis. I want to spend my time on the issues, especially those that are important, that I understand and that oftentimes only the ambassador can do."

Eliasson said he would have spent more time on management issues if he had to. "If I have an organization which is not well managed, I do something about it and very forcefully. I'm a navy officer. I can give orders, by God," he said.

A number of Swedish diplomats told me that the Washington embassy was the perfect size for Eliasson.

"The embassy here is the right scale for Jan. It has a broad range of activities, but it's small enough that Jan can deal with people individually and win them over with his charm, even as he is sometimes driving them crazy with his requests," a Swedish diplomat told me. "He's very demanding and he needed his personal charm to pull it off," he added.

The ambassador was assisted by his personal secretary, Monica Lundkvist, a good-humored, efficient, well-organized woman who often worked until late in the evening following up on Eliasson's projects. Eliasson wrote notes to himself at work and at home about projects he wanted done and would hand them over to Lundkvist for follow-up. She would arrange meetings, send out documents, and place phone calls. She would check to make sure the ambassador's personal calendar was consistent with the master diary that she kept.

The flow of phone calls into the ambassador's office was steady but not overwhelming. It would range between five and twenty-five a day. But Eliasson made a number of calls from his cell phone and often received returned calls at this number.

"He was always on the phone," an embassy staffer said.

Eliasson received a number of visitors from Sweden. Each month, he might have a dozen scheduled meetings with visiting businessmen or parliamentarians as well as occasional drop-by sessions with Swedes passing through Washington.

The ambassador rarely went anyplace without his Mont Blanc pen, using it to scrawl notes and mark up documents. When he misplaced his pen, Lundkvist often led the search team, combing the ambassador's office and calling his driver, Zigurs Liepins, to look through the ambassador's limousine. When all else failed, Lundkvist urged Eliasson to try to remember the last time he used the pen. This timeless strategy, employed by parents around the world, often worked.

Eliasson studied all the cables drafted by Swedish diplomats that would go out under his name, paying special attention to the section that listed assessments and recommendations. He would rework cables extensively until he was pleased with the final product.

"I read everything that goes out under my name, especially when it expresses a view," he said.

The ambassador urged his staff to be active in Washington, to meet with contacts in the administration, Congress, and the diplomatic corps, and to attend seminars and conferences.

"I tell my staff: 'Don't just sit there like shrinking violets. Be active. Make Sweden noticed. You're an actor not an observer. You go around once in life; you should make a difference. You should allow your own personal style to come out within our diplomatic style. You should let your charisma come out,'" he said. "I'm very proactive. I belong to the school that believes that embassies are growing more important. If you have good ambassadors you should give them more responsibility and power."

Eliasson says that he was willing to move ahead on a matter if it was time-sensitive and he was confident he knew the general direction Sweden's government supported. He acknowledged that he was sometimes more aggressive than some in Stockholm wanted.

"This is the most important bilateral embassy. We are definitely one of the most active embassies. Some people ask, 'What are you doing? You're not the foreign minister.'"

The embassy doesn't have a formal orientation program in Washington for newly arriving diplomats. Eliasson met with new diplomats when they arrived in Washington, outlining his views on diplomacy, his sense of Washington, and his expectations for their work. He made sure his social secretary put them on invitation lists so they could begin to meet key officials and understand the social aspects of their job. He urged people to set up meetings with him if they wanted to discuss their careers.

"I told people to see me if they want a discussion of their situation and development. I want to help them and their careers. This is an elite group. I try to promote them so that when they go home they are at a higher level. Almost everybody is promoted after Washington," he said.

The ambassador maintained an open-door policy and urged his staff to bring visitors by to meet with him.

"I always have my door open so people can drop in and they do. And it gives me a feel for what is going on. I don't like to sit behind a closed door. I want to feel the movement, the life in the embassy."

He sent his staff a barrage of notes and almost always returned memos with notes, questions, and even grammatical corrections. One Swedish diplomat told me that she doesn't recall sending Eliasson a memo in which he didn't find a typographical or grammatical mistake.

A self-professed technophobe, he would write out notes and memos by hand and have Lundkvist type them up and send them out. She also printed out his E-mails. She did teach him one important technical skill: how to delete E-mails.

Every fall he would hold a day-long retreat with his staff at his residence to discuss the next year's agenda. He would take their ideas, add his own, and put together a work plan that he would submit to Stockholm in November.

"Stockholm usually does what we suggest. It's good for morale. They shouldn't think they have a better idea of what is going on than we do," he said.

CHAPTER 16

The Mentor

Eliasson talks about modern art with some young visitors at his residence

৵ I ৵

It's an early spring morning in Washington, and the graduate students at the Johns Hopkins University's School of Advanced International Studies are gathering in a small classroom for Professor William Zartman's seminar on negotiation. Zartman is an internationally respected expert and has written a number of highly regarded books on the subject. But for this class, Zartman has been inviting some of the top negotiators in Washington to speak to his students. This morning's guest speaker is Jan Eliasson.

Eliasson, dressed in elegant blue pinstripes and a gold tie, strides into the room, swings by the coffee and doughnuts, and greets Zartman. As he banters with the professor, about a dozen students trickle into the classroom. Many of the students are dressed in blue-jean, baseball-hat casual.

After introducing the ambassador, Zartman asks the students to briefly describe their backgrounds and specific areas of interest for him. Eliasson watches the students as each one speaks, looking into their eyes, listening to their experiences, and jotting an occasional note.

An adamant opponent of early morning meetings, Eliasson makes a few self-deprecating quips about his persuasive skills in the morning. As the ambassador begins to speak, the students lean forward in their chairs. As students of negotiation they are about to hear from one who has done it successfully at the highest levels. While this morning's talk is about mediation, it's also more broadly about diplomacy and the value of solving disputes without violence and destruction.

The ambassador notes that certain core skills are important in diplomacy, including a grasp of history, geography, economics, and religious and cultural traditions. He gives a quick summary of his career, briefly describing his mediation experiences in the Iran-Iraq war, the dispute over Nagorno-Karabakh, and in Sudan. He then launches into what he calls a "very simple and very practical" primer on mediation, focusing on who mediates, when they mediate, and how they mediate.

Eliasson argues that the type of mediator depends on the particular circumstances of the dispute. Some disputes, such as the conflict between Israel and the Palestinians, are best addressed by the mediation of great powers such as the United States. Other disputes are best tackled by international organizations such as the United Nations, and cites the Iran-Iraq war in the 1980s as an example. Certain conflicts can be mediated by the good offices of small countries with a history of respect for international law such as Sweden and Norway. And some conflicts, such as civil wars, are best tackled by independent organizations such as the Carter Center or by former President Jimmy Carter himself.

Mediation, Eliasson says, should ideally occur when both sides are politically and militarily balanced—either equally strong or equally weak. He describes his experience during the Iran-Iraq war in the 1980s in which an agreement that was tentatively proposed in 1981 was accepted near the end of the decade—but only after seven hundred thousand Iraqis and Iranians had died, three million refugees were created, and staggering physical damage had occurred to both countries.

"It's important to seize the moment and persuade the parties that it's the right moment," he says. Eliasson relates this to one of the central challenges of diplomacy and mediation—timing.

"Never underestimate the importance of timing," he says. "I've seen proposals presented too early. The ground was not prepared."

In describing the craft of mediation, Eliasson stresses the importance of cultural sensitivity, careful use of language, and the overriding importance of truth, trust, and fairness. He recalls that during a negotiation between Iran and Iraq a member of his delegation spent the night studying the Koran, searching for a passage that would give religious legitimacy to the idea of Iran allowing Iraq to retreat from a part of Iran it had invaded. His colleague found a passage that urges Muslims not to attack someone who has his back to you.

Eliasson describes how he restarted a stalled negotiation between feuding Iranian factions by calling for a recess in the talks and asking to be taken to a carpet museum.

"I asked questions about the patterns and colors from different regions and by the time we returned to the negotiations I could feel that something had changed. There was a different atmosphere. I had shown an interest in their culture and their traditions and they began to see me as their friend, as someone who tried to understand them," he says.

The ambassador describes how a negotiation to end massive suffering in Sudan was revived when he set aside the concept of a cease-fire, which was unacceptable to the government because it was seen as conferring legitimacy to the insurgents, and used the idea of "humanitarian corridors" instead. This wordsmithing, Eliasson says, saved thousands of lives.

Finally, he emphasizes the need for honesty and credibility if the mediator is to have any chance. Without the trust of the affected parties no mediator will succeed, he says.

Eliasson tells the stories with humor, sophistication, historical context, and a blend of pride and self-deprecation. The students are in his pocket. They ask him informed and insightful questions—and appear to want the class to keep going.

Beyond offering a primer on mediation, Eliasson conveys his deep respect for the profession of diplomacy, emphasizes the need to practice it aggressively and creatively, and offers the conviction that done well diplomacy can save lives and help people that badly need help.

The ambassador listens as Sweden's Crown Princess Victoria meets with reporters

As we walk from the classroom to his office several blocks away, Eliasson is pleased, even buoyant about the session. He knows he inspired the students and the next generation of diplomats.

৯৯ II ৯৯

While in Washington, Eliasson relished opportunities to connect with bright and interested young people, whether students or interns or young professionals. While not all ambassadors assume the role of professor, it is one Eliasson enjoyed and embraced. A man interested in ideas and especially their practical application, he is comfortable in academic and university environments. A former lecturer at Uppsala University in Sweden, Eliasson likes to teach and to learn.

The ambassador enjoys connecting with young people, basking in the adulation and the chance to have an impact on lives.

"What students always remember are the examples. You can come up with lofty, beautiful principles, but it's the examples and images they remember. Images create such strong emotional reactions," he said.

"I feel very good when I see young people light up and I have given that light. There is so much desire for young people to do good and so much untapped energy and talent. I'm thinking more and more of mentoring. Maybe the most important thing I can do now is passing on as much as possible to the next generation of diplomats. After all, I've had nearly forty years of experience, and I believe in my profession. I've learned something about the trade during my years."

Eliasson said he made it a priority to schedule an hour-long meeting with new interns at the Swedish embassy and used the meeting to describe his career, discuss Sweden's diplomatic traditions, and answer their questions. He brought interns along to conferences and meetings when appropriate. He urged them to consider diplomacy as a career and to have large ambitions.

He said his commitment to reach out to the young was partly the result of his own experiences as an exchange student in the United States. When he visited Washington and attended an event at the Swedish embassy, an older diplomat spoke with him extensively and was kind and generous.

"I've never forgotten that. It was so important to me," he said.

৯৯ III ৯৯

Several months later, on a hot, oppressive July afternoon, Jan Eliasson is on Capitol Hill, invited by Democratic Congressman Tom Lantos to speak to about two hundred congressional interns about Raoul Wallenberg.

Lantos, who was nearly killed in Hungary during the Nazi occupation during World War II, has been a tireless champion of Wallenberg. He's successfully lobbied to have him honored on a postage stamp and made an honorary American citizen. He even pressed hard to have a bust of Wallenberg displayed in the U.S. Capitol and often takes visitors to look at it.

For the past several years, Lantos has asked Eliasson to speak about Wallenberg to Capitol Hill interns as well as to Congress's Human Rights Caucus. Eliasson knows Wallenberg's history and can speak about him in a compelling way, linking his personal bravery to decisions we all faces in our lives.

After preliminary remarks about Wallenberg, Lantos introduces the ambassador, lavishing praise on Eliasson as "the most highly regarded person in Sweden's diplomatic service" and a "great scholar of Wallenberg."

The annual trip to Capitol Hill to speak about Wallenberg is one that Eliasson relishes. It allows him to describe one of Sweden's moral giants to an impressionable audience of interested Americans.

On this afternoon, eager, clean-scrubbed young people are packed into almost every seat in the wood-paneled hearing room usually used by the House Science Committee. Dapper and polished, Eliasson is commanding and passionate about Wallenberg and the lessons his life offers to the young.

"I'm moved to be here with you. I'm also moved because you are here, because you represent the future," Eliasson says as he begins to tell the story of Wallenberg's life, which included architecture studies at the University of Michigan and an aspiring career in international trade.

In March of 1944, Nazi Germany invaded Hungary and began to exterminate the country's large Jewish population. Wallenberg went to Budapest as a diplomat in the Swedish embassy. Horrified at the slaughter, Wallenberg frantically worked to protect as many people as he could. He designed a Swedish protective pass, called the Schutz-pass, which had no value in international law but gave some Hungarian Jews protection. He also set up about thirty Swedish safe houses that Wallenberg declared as Swedish territory. He even pulled Jews from trains headed to concentration camps, threatening Nazis with postwar punishment if they did not let the Jews leave with him as protected Swedish citizens.

Wallenberg saved thousands of Hungarian Jews from certain death. In January 1945 the invading Soviet army took him into custody and he was never heard from again. Eliasson describes Wallenberg as a "suave and elegant diplomat" who saw a great evil and confronted it without reservations or hesitations. Wallenberg, the ambassador declares, is a reminder that one person with courage can make a difference. Even when the world seemed hopelessly dark, he offered hope and help and saved thousands of people.

"When you face evil, there is no choice. There is no decision-making process when facing evil," Eliasson says to the rapt audience. "You can all make a difference. You must never give up. There is always a way."

Eliasson linked Wallenberg's work to his own convictions about the need for preventive diplomacy.

"We must act early. When you see a disaster looming, go for it. It's not always rewarded in public life or in the media," he says, adding that the world's failure to act in Bosnia, Cambodia, and Sudan is a sad legacy for humanity.

And he concludes with his signature call to arms.

"Without passion nothing happens," the ambassador says. "Without compassion the wrong things happen."

When the session is over, a dozen interns crowd around Eliasson, asking him questions, posing with him for photos. Most of them take brochures about Wallenberg before going back to their offices.

CHAPTER 17

Sweden on the Potomac

Eliasson and the late Sweden foreign minister, Anna Lindh, at the site of Sweden's new embassy in Washington, DC

ҩ I ҩ

In June of 2003, Sweden's foreign minister, Anna Lindh, visited Washington for several days of meetings. On her first morning in Washington, she and Jan Eliasson hosted a small press briefing, held a staff meeting, visited the State Department; and then, before going to Martin's, a Georgetown restaurant, for a cheeseburger lunch, they stopped at the site of the new Swedish embassy along the north shore of the Potomac River.

A photograph from that visit conveys many moods. Lindh, her jacket draped over her shoulder, is squinting into the warm and bright Washington sunshine. Eliasson, gesturing with a sweep of his arm, appears to be outlining an ambitious scheme to a polite, interested, but slightly skeptical recipient. But Eliasson himself looks ambivalent and uncertain, almost hesitant.

The events culminating in Sweden's decision to build a spectacular, gleaming, glass box of an embassy along the shores of the Potomac are tangled and complex with twists and turns, soaring ambitions and false starts. In one of his final speeches in Washington, Eliasson quipped that of the many daunting negotiations he's been involved in during his long diplomatic career, those involving the new embassy, the House of Sweden, were among the most difficult.

"I was very involved in negotiations involving Iran and Iraq and I would put the difficulty of the negotiations of the House of Sweden in that category," he said with a playful touch of hyperbole.

Government agencies in both Stockholm and Washington were deeply involved in the project, as were architects, diplomats, political leaders, developers, brokers—and the ambassador. Sweden's decision to build a new Washington embassy reflected a desire to leave behind a downtown office building that was pleasant but nondescript. It was also an aggressive and expensive decision to reposition Sweden and sell it as a modern, forward-leaning country in the political capital of the world. The design of the new embassy was meant to convey openness, transparency, and confidence in an increasingly hunkered-down and barricaded Washington. It was conceived of and created for one central reason: to bring attention to Sweden.

"Sweden's embassies and other overseas properties are the face of our country abroad," Sweden's National Property Board, the lead agency planning the new embassy, proclaims on its Web site.

"They show off Sweden to the world and aim to reflect Swedish culture, design, traditions and quality. They should also reflect and represent Swedish trade. Visiting a Swedish embassy should convey an impression of meeting the very soul of Sweden."

৵ II ৵

Sweden's political leaders and diplomats have been confounded and conflicted for more than a quarter of a century about what kind of physical presence they wanted in Washington. In 1950, the Swedish government purchased a spectacular Spanish-mission-style mansion in northwest Washington for the residence of the ambassador. Built in 1923 by architect Arthur B. Heaton for David Lawrence, founder of *US News & World Report,* the mansion is surrounded by several acres of beautiful lawns and gardens and has a tennis court. The government bought it for $160,000. It's now worth more than $20 million.

Sweden had looked around for several decades for a permanent embassy to conduct official business. Swedish diplomats worked out of a mansion on R Street off Embassy Row, and then spent almost a quarter of a century at the Watergate building. For the past decade, Sweden has used the top two floors of an office building in downtown Washington as its chancery.

While reasonably comfortable, Sweden's embassy in a downtown Washington office building doesn't convey anything about Sweden in a city where appearances matter. In fact, Swedish diplomats were embarrassed that they didn't have their own chancery.

Eliasson joins Washington, DC Mayor Anthony Williams, developer Alan Novak, and others at the groundbreaking for the new embassy. Novak's wife, Kate, was a longtime advocate of an embassy on the Potomac.

"We were the only the country in the European Union to have an embassy in an office building," Eliasson said.

Count Wilhelm Wachtmeister, Sweden's ambassador to the United States for fifteen years, tried during much of the 1980s to get approval to build a new Swedish embassy on Massachusetts Avenue. The proposal cleared several major procedural hurdles, but was eventually derailed when it lost a zoning battle in 1993.

Another of Eliasson's predecessors, Henrik Liljegren, was captivated by the idea of building an embassy on the Potomac and found a suitable location on the Georgetown waterfront. But the idea stalled and appeared to die when he left Washington in 1997.

At that time, Eliasson, as the deputy foreign minister, opposed the proposal to build an embassy on the Potomac River because of concerns about flooding and because the proposal involved selling Sweden's Nebraska Avenue ambassadorial residence.

Eliasson's immediate predecessor, Rolf Ekeus, expressed displeasure with Sweden's seeming interminable struggle to build an embassy it could be proud of in Washington.

"We have one of the oldest diplomatic relationships with America, dating back to Ben Franklin, but never had a permanent embassy chancery," he lamented.

ৡ III ৡ

When Eliasson arrived in Washington in 2000, the idea of building a new embassy was still being debated in Stockholm. The Swedish government had constructed state-of-the-art embassies in Tokyo and Berlin and felt these buildings sent a positive message about Sweden and its place in the world.

A revamped proposal to build an embassy on the same property along the Potomac that Liljegren suggested was now more compelling to the Swedish government and Eliasson because new technologies sharply reduced the dangers of flooding. Additionally, the new proposal did not include selling the ambassador's residence, which Eliasson believed was an important feature of Sweden's Washington presence.

With Washington as the world's only superpower, nations from around the world have been scrambling to build glittering, impressive embassies in the city. In the last decade, more than a dozen countries have built or are in the midst of building embassies. While the new embassies differ in structure and scale, virtually all try to convey a compelling image of their country and to gain notice in Washington.

Finland, Sweden's Scandinavian friend and rival, opened a sleek embassy in 1994 that has captured the imagination of Washington. Located on Massachusetts Avenue, across from the vice president's home, the Finnish embassy is a compelling Washington cultural center with programs and exhibits that attract visitors throughout the year.

When Eliasson hosted a reception in 2002 to announce that Sweden would open a new embassy on the Potomac, his words conveyed a sweeping sense of history and a gentle sense of competition.

"This is the most powerful country in the history of the world and we need a showpiece for Sweden," he said. "Like the Finnish embassy," he added.

৯৯ IV ৯৯

The Swedish government commissioned the Swedish Property Board to build a House of Sweden in Washington. A competition for design proposals was announced in June 2002 and the winning architects were chosen in January 2003 by a panel of judges that included Eliasson. The judges met for six days to consider five proposals.

The winning architects were Gert Wingårdh and Tomas Hansen who summarized the embassy's theme as refined simplicity. They said it conveys the essence of Swedish design with a clear sense of openness and creative sensibility in the use of materials. The proposal was a modernistic glass box, which is encompassed by an intricate belt of wood.

"The transparency of the building will reflect Sweden's desire for openness and dialogue in the most important capital in the world. Our embassy serves not only as a place for Sweden's representatives to work, but also an arena for the exchange of culture and ideas," Eliasson said when the winning design was selected.

The embassy building not only houses the normal chancery functions, but also includes premises for exhibitions, seminars, and other activities open to the public. Sixteen corporate apartments would be rented out, primarily to companies with Swedish ties.

A review of the embassy in the *Washington Post* said the new embassy could become "an instant landmark, a simple yet sophisticated symbol of internationalism and openness on one of Washington's loveliest and most visible sights."

乸 **V** 乸

The U.S. Commission of Fine Arts regularly receives presentations on building proposals from architects and developers, but almost never sees an ambassador. It did on the morning of April 22, 2003. Eliasson traveled to Washington's National Building Museum to attend a meeting of the commission, a group whose approval was needed for the House of Sweden to go forward.

The commission was established by Congress in 1910 as an independent agency to advise the federal and District of Columbia governments on matters of art and architecture that affect the appearance of the nation's capital. The commission's primary role is to advise on proposed public building projects, but it also reviews private buildings adjacent to public buildings and grounds of major importance such as Rock Creek Park and projects in the historic division of Georgetown.

On this morning, the seven commissioners sat around a rectangular table at the front of the room, while the ambassador sat in the audience with the team that was charged to present Sweden's proposal to the commission. The team included Peter Ohrstedt, a senior official with the Swedish National Property Board; architect Tomas Hansen; and Gregory Hunt, dean of the School of Architecture at Catholic University and chairman of the panel that chose the winning design.

After Ohrstedt, Hansen, and Hunt outlined the technical and architectural aspects of the proposal, Eliasson was called upon to conclude the presentation. Rising from his seat in the front row, Eliasson offered brief remarks that blended global politics, Swedish history, Washington's architectural traditions, and his own experiences in the United States.

He said that Sweden's connection to American waterfronts began more than three hundred and fifty years earlier when Sweden established a colony on the shores of Delaware in 1638.

"I'm a Navy officer myself and the very fact that we now seem to be on our way to building at the Potomac brings back that historic link between our two countries, but in a deeper sense brings in the element of the United States and Europe belonging together. We have had some strains in that relationship recently but I think there is a need for a reminder of the links between our countries and not least Europe and the United States," he said.

He observed that he served as first secretary in the Swedish embassy in the early '70s when Sweden left an Embassy Row house on R Street because it was too small. Sweden, he said, has been looking for many years to find the right place to call home. And it found that place.

"It is important to have a presence in Washington," he said. The embassy building that was being proposed would be Sweden's contribution to the beauty of Washington, he said, adding that he was very impressed by how carefully the city—and the commission—worked to ensure that appropriate structures are built in historic areas of the city.

"Ever since I served here in the '70s I've been impressed by how careful you are in making sure that buildings that are accepted in your city fit into the environment, both historically and, of course, aesthetically. We are very humbled knowing that we are in this area with the national monuments in the neighborhood and the Kennedy Center," he said.

The ambassador concluded by saying that he was grateful for the chance to appear "in front of this august body and ask for your continued understanding and, hopefully, support of this project, which we hope will be a link between our two countries." The commission approved the Swedish proposal a few minutes later.

Several weeks later, Eliasson received a letter from Harry Robinson, chairman of the commission, noting that the panel appreciated his appearance and found the proposal excellent. He described the concept of the embassy as "elegantly uncomplicated but rich in detail." And he said that Sweden was going to make a very positive contribution to Washington's architecture.

"It has the potential to create a building that is worthy of this prominent site on the north bank of the Potomac River and it seems to have the character that is essential to hold its own in the context of the John F. Kennedy Center, the Watergate complex, and the other national memorials along the waterfront," Robinson wrote.

❧ VI ❧

The official groundbreaking ceremony for the House of Sweden was held on April 23, 2004. Eliasson and Marita Ulvskog, Sweden's minister for culture, were joined by Washington Mayor Anthony Williams and Alan Novak, a Washington developer who was a long-time advocate for building a Swedish embassy on the Potomac. As the construction of the House of Sweden began, Eliasson and his staff, especially Peter Wahlquist, the cultural counselor, held long brainstorming sessions about the best way to present the new embassy and its programs in Washington.

"The inauguration of the House of Sweden in the autumn of 2006 will be a milestone in the relationship between Sweden and the United States," an embassy memo said. "The House of Sweden will be a showcase for

Sweden on the Potomac in the political capital of the world and an arena for meetings between Sweden and the United States. We are working on events with strong Swedish themes such as architecture and design, healthy life style, transportation and communications, innovation, water and environment, children's literature, the Nobel prizes, youth culture, security and Swedish food culture," it continued.

The new embassy would depict Sweden as a modern and progressive society that is highly transparent, outwardly focused, and environmentally aware. It would also substantially increase the visibility of Sweden in Washington.

"The House of Sweden—with the new Swedish embassy—will place Sweden in a spectacular position to make its flag seen in a city with more than 170 embassies," the embassy memo declared.

Jane C. Loeffler, an architectural historian at the University of Maryland, said the new Swedish embassy is an ambitious project that is certain to have long-term ramifications in defining the Swedish presence in Washington.

"What Sweden is doing is unusual and bold. It is also a sign of Swedish optimism that the embassy will include public-access facilities as well as residences. The extensive use of glass is certainly a sign of optimism and openness as well. The riverfront site is a prominent one. No other embassies are located along the Potomac. The move to that site is comparable to Canada's move to the foot of Capitol Hill, a high profile area that had not previously been used for embassy offices.

"Just as Canada selected that site to underscore its close relationship to the United States, Sweden is doing the same in creating this new Georgetown landmark. It looks as if the building will be used as a showcase for Swedish projects. It will also draw attention to Sweden as a forward-looking, innovative, and design-aware place. Following in the footsteps of Finland, the Swedes are obviously planning to use the structure to make a statement about their nation and what it represents."

But she said there is hard work ahead.

"You can have the best embassy in the world, but if you don't have programs that bring people in and tell them about your country you haven't accomplished that much," she said.

֍ VII ֍

While Eliasson was not the central figure in the drive to create a new embassy, he was far more than the "engaged onlooker" he self-depreciatingly suggests. During his tenure in Washington he spent progressively more time on the House of Sweden. The ambassador said the House of Sweden is part of a conscious effort to market Sweden in a more aggressive way in Washington and the United States. The House of Sweden, he said, is part of a broader effort to intensify Sweden's cultural diplomacy. He pressed his staff to develop programs so Sweden could take advantage of the new embassy.

"One of the problems I've worried about is that you get money for the building and infrastructure, but you don't get money for activities. I've been telling everybody that if you have this showcase you better have something to show," he said.

Eliasson's work on the new embassy arose from a passion to see Sweden represented in the United States in the most favorable light. He was fully aware that he would not be around to reap the benefits. The ambassador said the deliberations in Stockholm and the negotiations in Washington regarding the House of Sweden were exhaustive and often exhausting. No decision seemed final. He said he began warning in 2002 that the new embassy would cost more than first anticipated, as fees for consultants and others mounted.

In the face of these rising costs, the Finance Ministry in late 2003 resurrected the idea of selling the Nebraska Avenue residence to help offset the rising costs. Eliasson spent a month scrambling to derail that idea, working the phones and all angles in Stockholm to keep the residence. He succeeded.

"I've been fighting so hard for this residence, fighting for the chancery, fighting for the programs that will be shown in 2006 and 2007. I think I have a responsibility. You should not only think of yourself," he said.

The ambassador said that watching a Swedish embassy rise on the shores of the Potomac was gratifying for him, especially as a former Navy officer who loves water.

"It's a very concrete accomplishment to see that building grow. It has been such a headache. I've had to fight so many battles. But once that building is there no one will regret it. We will be the only embassy on the water— Sweden on the Potomac."

CHAPTER **18**

Sweden, Inc.

Eliasson, and his successor Gunnar Lund, and Caroline Vicini work with Swedish businesses.

ꝏ I ꝏ

In the spring of 2004, Jan Eliasson made the kind of phone call that ambassadors dream of making: he called an important senator to tell him that a large company from his country was going to make a large investment in the senator's state. Eliasson called Senator Paul Sarbanes, a Democrat from

157

Maryland and a senior member of the Senate's Banking and Foreign Relations committees, to tell him that Volvo had decided to invest $150 million to expand a factory in Hagerstown.

Volvo had considered making the investment in several other states and Mexico, but finally decided to upgrade its Hagerstown facility, which had manufactured Mack engines since 1961. The Volvo Group is the world's largest producer of heavy-duty diesel engines. The investment was designed to transform the Hagerstown facility into the North American Center for Excellence for power train operations of the Volvo Group.

Volvo officials informed Eliasson as soon as the decision was made and allowed him to make the call to tell Sarbanes—a call that made Sarbanes's day.

"I had no trouble getting through to the senator that day. He was very eager to hear the good news," Eliasson says with a chuckle.

While the ambassador was not the pivotal actor in the negotiations resulting in Volvo's decision, his role was subtle but important. Eliasson followed Volvo's deliberations closely, made calls to Volvo executives to learn what they were thinking, passed on information to Sarbanes and other Maryland leaders, and even offered his residence as the venue for an important Volvo reception.

Volvo decided to hold its international annual board meeting in Washington on October 2, 2002, and that night Eliasson hosted a reception for the company's senior executives and American business and government leaders. He invited Maryland's congressional delegation to attend and most came, including Sarbanes. The lawmakers had a pleasant evening talking with Volvo executives in a relaxed setting and got a better sense of what the company's needs and concerns were.

In the end Volvo's decision to invest in Maryland was driven by bottom-line factors, including the state of Maryland's $5.7 million package of grants and loans. There was also a crucial agreement with United Auto Workers. In exchange for Volvo's investment and commitment to increase engine output at Hagerstown, the union agreed to allow a number of functions to be outsourced to other companies, or other Volvo plants, that could do them for a lower cost.

Eliasson served as a conduit of information, a convener of helpful meetings, and a sort of a chaperone who made sure the parties understood each other and were speaking the same language.

Several months after the announcement was made, Eliasson traveled to Hagerstown for the October ceremony to celebrate the decision. He shared the dais with Maryland Governor Bob Ehrlich and a host of government and company officials. One of the special guests was the deputy director of the Environmental Protection Agency, Stephen Johnson, who later became the agency's director. Volvo officials said that Johnson said he would attend the event when he was told that the ambassador was a confirmed speaker for the ceremony. This gave the event credibility and significance.

"I don't get that much involved in concrete cases. But I'm proud of what I did with Senator Sarbanes. We were instrumental in bringing Volvo to Hagerstown," Eliasson says.

❧ II ❧

One of the truisms of modern diplomacy is that ambassadors and the embassies they preside over are getting more involved in economic issues. If ambassadors are becoming less central in the diplomacy of high-profile political negotiations, they are becoming more active in the diplomacy of commerce and culture.

But the role of the ambassador in business and commerce is often misunderstood. They rarely negotiate investment deals or craft trade agreements. Instead, they serve more as conveners or hosts, setting up meetings, making introductions, placing phone calls, and then stepping aside to let companies conduct their negotiations and consummate their deals.

Foreign ministries across the world are getting more active in promoting the exports of firms, helping secure business alliances, and encouraging investment toward their home nations. The Swedish Foreign Ministry says that one of its chief responsibilities is to help Swedish firms find and conduct business overseas. It believes that all business promotion, which includes support of exports, investments, and tourism, contributes to the government's overall objective of increasing economic growth and employment in Sweden.

The Swedish Foreign Ministry places its global network of embassies and consulates and the expertise of its diplomats at the disposal of the Swedish business sector. The Foreign Ministry works in close collaboration with others, including the Swedish Trade Council, the Invest in Sweden Agency, the Swedish Institute, the Swedish Travel and Tourism Council, the Swedish Federation of Trade, the Confederation of Swedish Enterprise, and the chambers of commerce in Sweden and abroad.

The Swedish Trade Council, which has offices in forty countries, is responsible for the majority of practical assistance given to Swedish companies. The primary role of embassies and consulates general in markets where the Swedish Trade Council has facilities is to demonstrate official support and to participate in more general types of campaigns. In markets where the Swedish Trade Council does not maintain an office of its own, embassies

The new Swedish embassy is designed to help promote Swedish products and services.

and consulates general look after commercial interests, often through the work of special trade departments.

Sweden's diplomatic network is charged to monitor political and economic developments overseas and to look for business opportunities for private sector firms. It offers start-up services for Swedish firms, helps run visitors' programs, and monitors procurement opportunities offered by multilateral institutions that Sweden contributes to, such as the World Bank, the European Union, and the United Nations, to make sure Swedish firms are considered. Additionally, Swedish diplomats are expected to place their personal network of business and political contacts at the disposal of Swedish firms and engage in the general promotion of Sweden.

ఞ III ఞ

The Washington embassy under Eliasson's leadership monitored the American economic and business climate, looking for trade and investment opportunities for Swedish firms. But it didn't typically get involved in specific cases; this was largely the realm of the Swedish Trade Council, which has an office in New York.

The Invest in Sweden Agency, also with a branch in New York, is a government agency that provides free information and contact services for foreign investors evaluating investment opportunities in Sweden. The ISA provides specific information about key industrial and service sectors in Sweden and detailed briefings about national, regional, and local business conditions there. It also helps businesses find suitable locations in Sweden, possible Swedish partners, contacts with government agencies at all levels, and lists of lawyers, accountants, and recruitment companies.

Swedish firms operating in the United States are typically experienced and sophisticated and know what market they are trying to penetrate. The very active Swedish American Chambers of Commerce (SACC) in the United States has nineteen regional affiliates. The Washington affiliate of the SACC was based at the embassy during Eliasson's tenure and its staffers were invited to attend embassy staff meetings. The Swedish embassy worked with SACC on the annual Entrepreneurial Days conference in Washington, which is the most visible trade event between the United States and Sweden.

Eliasson spoke frequently before business groups, usually giving a broad overview of Swedish American relations and praising the skill of Swedish businesses. He hosted events at his residence where business leaders from Sweden could mingle with American government officials. For example, in 2003, the Swedish pharmaceutical company AstraZeneca wanted to get access to some top business leaders attending the BIO-Windhover conference in Washington. The conference was difficult to get into so Eliasson decided to invite the participants to his residence for a dinner.

"Not many people say no to a dinner invitation to an ambassador's residence," said Eric Enroth of the Invest in Sweden Agency. "So we had a very good attendance."

AstraZeneca and ISA officials were able to meet with the business leaders they were having difficulty tracking down.

The ambassador also tried to keep a close eye on the burgeoning American homeland security market that surged after September 11, 2001. The embassy hosted a conference on American homeland security programs in Washington, which a number of Swedish firms attended as did United States government officials and business executives. He was concerned that since Sweden doesn't have a comparable agency, opportunities for Swedish firms to bid for contracts could go unexploited.

But Eliasson didn't spend as much time on economic issues as some ambassadors do. He was available to help when needed, received regular briefings from his staff, met with Swedish business leaders visiting Washington, and made crucial calls when he felt his voice was relevant and might be effective. Enroth said he called on Eliasson to help on various occasions.

"Jan was always willing to help, but we used our access to him carefully. He's a diplomat and as a diplomat he was a door opener—and the door he opened was to his beautiful residence. When the ambassador calls, almost everyone will answer or return the call. And almost everyone accepts an invitation to come to the ambassador's residence," he said

Christopher Wall, a Washington lawyer who was the chairman of the Swedish American Chamber of Commerce, said Eliasson understood the connection between commerce and diplomacy.

"Jan's a pure diplomat, even a classic diplomat. But he's also a modern diplomat. He focused on security and politics, but he was more than willing to help out Swedish companies and Swedish businesses. Some of his predecessors had absolutely no interest in economic issues. That wasn't true with Jan. He didn't spend 80 percent of his time on these issues, more like 20 percent. But he was ready to help—with a speech, with a call, with an inquiry," Wall said. "He recognized that on some issues a call from the embassy and especially the ambassador was important and would be taken seriously."

Geoff Merrill, an executive with Volvo Group North America, says his company kept in close touch with the embassy.

"It's a big advantage for Volvo to be associated with the embassy. People in Washington have a lot of respect for Sweden and Swedish diplomats. When they call a government agency, the call is usually returned," he said. "You don't bring in the ambassador on day-to-day matters. That's a waste of his time. We deal with his staff—who are very good. We use the ambassador for high-level contacts—and he's very good."

෨ IV ෨

Eliasson described Sweden's active involvement in the global economy as a metaphor for, and a manifestation of, its involvement in global affairs. The World Economic Forum in 2004 ranked Sweden in third place after Finland and the United States in its survey of 104 countries and their capacity for growth in the medium term. With a domestic market of only nine million people, Swedish firms need to export to survive. And Sweden is home to a number of multinationals that are significant global companies—Volvo,

SAAB, Ericsson, Electrolux, ABB, AstraZeneca, Pharmacia, SCA, Scania, and Securitas.

Swedish firms are well represented in Fortune's List of the Global 500 and Forbes' Global 2000, a list of the world's biggest companies. In 2005, Sweden had more companies on the Forbes list (twenty-eight), than most other European Union countries. For example, of the twenty-five EU member states, the United Kingdom had one hundred and forty, Germany had sixty-three, France had sixty-two, Italy had forty-five, the Netherlands had thirty-seven, and Spain had thirty. Sweden had almost as many as Finland, Denmark, and Norway combined.

Sweden is a leader in a newer phenomenon: consumer-goods companies such as IKEA and Hennes & Mauritz, which are popular in the United States. Sweden is also home to growing industries in areas such as information technology, telecommunications, biomedicine, and medical research.

Sweden also takes pride in being at the vanguard of a new sector that includes design, fashion, music, architecture, and gastronomy: the so-called experience industry.

Eliasson often emphasized the important links between the American and Swedish economies. He noted that the United States is the most important market for Sweden. Swedish exports of goods and services reached $161 billion in 2003. More than two hundred fifty thousand Americans are employed by Swedish firms; more than one hundred thousand Swedes are employed by U.S. companies in Sweden. Twenty-two Swedish firms have set up research institutions in the United States; seventeen American firms are doing advanced research in Sweden. Fully 20 percent of Swedish foreign direct investment goes to the United States; of all foreign direct investment coming into Sweden, a quarter comes from the United States.

V

Eliasson was deeply involved with Sweden's defense industry, which is substantial but with a limited domestic market, so it has to export to survive. The United States is the largest consumer of defense products and services in the world. While the United State's defense procurement policy is highly regulated and structured, it is also an area in which political contacts are considered crucial.

"The defense industry requires contacts high up. There are also sometimes political actors involved," Eliasson said. "I was very much involved with the defense industry. They're often asking for my help. I believe my major job is to build up a very strong network—a network of contacts at the highest level."

Sweden's defense industry is technologically advanced in such areas as electronic warfare, signature management, underwater warfare, avionics, weapons systems, and ballistic protection. Its various systems and subsystems are increasingly purchased by, or developed in collaboration with, European and U.S. defense companies.

Sweden's Washington embassy has an office of defense industry cooperation, which is funded by the government and the defense industry. Its purpose is to support the Swedish defense-related industry in the United States.

The embassy works closely with a group of Swedish defense-related companies established in the United States, including Bofors Defense, Ericsson, FLIR Systems, MacGregor, SAAB, Nexplo, and SweDish. The embassy also has a master list of more than forty Swedish companies with a potential interest in the American defense market.

Eliasson said the embassy's job is to help Swedish defense firms find opportunities and compete for business in the American market. The embassy emphasized to Swedish firms that penetrating the American market required more than just a good product. Swedish firms also needed to understand the importance of U.S. trade barriers, the export control system, and the politics of defense procurement.

❧ VI ❧

Sven-Olof Hökborg, president of SAAB Technologies, said Eliasson was a significant asset for Sweden's defense-related community in Washington.

"Jan was very interested in the military, knows a lot about the military, and understands the needs of the military. He was willing to use his high-level contacts to help the Swedish defense industry," he said.

Eliasson said that one of his central goals was to make sure that Sweden's Gripen fighter aircraft was allowed to compete on a "level playing field" with the United States' F-16 and F-18. The Gripen is expected to be the backbone of the Swedish air force for many years to come. Because of its advanced technology and continuing export potential, the Gripen is the main driving force in Sweden's aviation industry.

"The Gripen is very important to Sweden. It was important for me to make sure it was well understood in the United States and allowed to compete, even against American systems," Eliasson says. "We didn't expect any special favors. We just wanted the chance to compete."

CHAPTER 19

Connecting with Culture
and Philanthropy

Jan and Kerstin Eliasson attend a ceremony with Lenape Indians

ৡ I ৡ

On a spectacular June evening in 2001, Jan and Kerstin Eliasson, joined by
Sweden's Princess Christina, hosted six hundred guests in the ambassador's residence for a midsummer night—Swedish style. The Eliassons had agreed to

host one of the signature events in Washington's social season: the Washington Opera Ball. This ball, held each summer, brings together the leaders of Washington's diplomatic, governmental, corporate, and arts communities to raise funds for the National Opera.

Washington's diplomatic community is integral to the event. In 2001, twenty-seven ambassadors hosted private dinners of between fifteen and twenty guests at their residences. Then about 10 p.m., all the partygoers converged at the Swedish residence for a late evening of dessert and dancing.

Visitors entered through the front door of the residence, passed through elegant rooms that were resplendent with yellow and blue floral arrangements, and then entered the backyard where a massive white tent transported everyone to a summer evening in Sweden.

"We are happy to host this historic ball on this magical, thoroughly enchanting summer evening," Eliasson told the assembled guests from a stage. He praised the Washington Opera for helping to "keep music and culture alive" in the city. Around midnight Eliasson reminded everyone that the sun rarely sets in Sweden during the summer. "Back in Stockholm right now it's still sunshine," he mused.

The Eliassons with King Carl Gustav XVI's sister, Princess Christina, and her husband Thord, led the revelers in dancing until the wee hours of the morning. Not only did Sweden help the Opera Ball raise $2 million that evening, but the Eliassons played host to some of Washington's most important people. Ambling through their backyard, for example, was a majority of the Supreme Court—Justices Stephen Breyer, Ruth Bader Ginsburg, Anthony Kennedy, Sandra Day O'Connor, and Antonin Scalia. And a number of powerful senators were at the ambassador's residence: John Breaux of Louisiana, Ted Stevens of Alaska, Robert Bennett of Utah, and Richard Shelby of Alabama.

The Sweden's Midsummer Evening soirée was described in glowing terms by the *Washington Post*.

"Old money, new money, diplomats and politicians all converged under a tent in Eliasson's garden, where they air-kissed, packed the dance floor and stayed up way past Washington's typical bedtime."

ℬ II ℬ

Usually when diplomats mention strategic decisions, they are referring to matters of broad political, security, or economic consequences. But Jan Eliasson has a more expansive definition. Hosting the 2001 Washington Opera Ball was, he said, a "strategic decision." It was also, he added, a "long-term investment."

When the embassy was approached by the Washington Opera in the fall of 2000 about hosting its annual fund-raising event in the spring of 2001, Eliasson and his wife immediately viewed it as a unique chance to put Sweden on Washington's social map and solidify its reputation as a generous and attractive country. After consulting with Stockholm, Eliasson agreed to be the main host for the ball. The Washington Opera took care of all expenses and organizational details. Sweden provided use of the residence and suggested ways to infuse the evening with a Swedish atmosphere.

For the ambassador, the decision to sponsor the ball had both cultural and pragmatic motivations. Both he and his wife love music and opera and wanted to support the Washington Opera. But it was also a good opportunity to get plugged in to an important part of Washington life. The Washington Opera is supported by the city's social, business, and political elite. Because of the Opera Ball experience, the Eliassons developed both strong friendships and casual contacts that stayed with them for the rest of their time in Washington.

Washington's cultural and philanthropic communities draw heavily on the diplomatic community, which has elegant residences, cultivated and polished hosts, and often the willingness to support charities in the community. This support is motivated by a blend of benevolent and tactical considerations. Supporting charities puts embassies on the social pages, gains them attention in Washington, and supports laudable causes.

Gunilla Stone said the Swedish embassy is approached frequently during the course of the year to sponsor or cosponsor events with charities.

"It's expected from the diplomatic community in Washington to participate. We try to do a few a year," she said.

The embassy typically agreed to host small dinners of about sixteen guests before the CARE Ball in the Spring, the Opera Ball in the summer, and the Meridian Ball in the fall. And then Eliasson and his wife, working with Stone, selected a few other smaller charities the embassy would support. Stone said the embassy's budget allowed it to host between five and seven smaller events a year for nonprofit organizations. For groups with modest resources, the embassy would charge either no fee or only a modest fee. For those seeking a more elaborate event, the embassy would charge for food and drinks.

๒ III ๒

On a cool March night, Eliasson hosted at his residence several dozen guests who were attending a fund-raising event of the Appleseed Foundation. The foundation's mission is to improve society through legal advocacy, community activism, and policy expertise. It works locally to address basic problems and produce practical, systemic solutions. The foundation believes that change is made best at the local level. Nationally, the foundation's role is to organize, support, and connect local Appleseed Centers.

The DC Appleseed Center for Law and Justice is an independent non-profit advocacy group that works with volunteer teams of attorneys and other experts to identify local public policy problems and find solutions. It's involved in a range of issues from improving the way the district manages polluted storm water runoff to fashioning a better system of governance for public schools.

The goal of this evening's reception is to raise funds for the Washington branch of the foundation. One of the members of the board approached Eliasson's daughter Anna who asked her father about hosting an event. Eliasson agreed to host the reception. The embassy offered use of the residence for several hours, picked up the costs of the drinks and food, and the ambassador played the role of host and toastmaster.

After unfurling his standard quips about Swedish weather, the residence's Spanish-mission style, and his wife's senior position in the government, Eliasson praised the work of the Appleseed Foundation. Buried deep in a pamphlet in the package of materials the foundation sent him, a line that the ambassador found seized his imagination and became the theme of his remarks. He read it slowly and with emphasis: "To listen to unheard voices, to uncover injustices, to win battles that no one else fights."

"To me," he said after a long pause, "that is poetry." The room erupted in applause. He concluded his remarks by recalling a statement made by Martin Luther centuries earlier: even if he knew the world would end the next day he would still plant his apple tree as a testament to hope for the future.

Again, applause. And connection.

৪৯ IV ৪৯

Jan Eliasson loves music and art; they are integral to his concept of balanced life. He also believes culture can be an important tool of diplomacy. During his tenure as ambassador, Eliasson invited a number of Swedish artists to his residence for receptions and to perform. And he attended concerts featuring Swedish artists. For example, he and his wife joined the king and queen for a concert at the Kennedy Center where the Swedish Radio Symphony Orchestra, the Swedish Radio Choir, and the Eric Ericsson Chamber Choir gave a performance of Verdi's *Requiem*. They were joined in the presidential box by Condoleezza Rice and World Bank president Jim Wolfensohn.

And he and his wife joined Richard Solomon and his wife one night in Washington's Blues Alley to listen to a Swedish jazz group. The musicians were surprised and flattered to be greeted by the ambassador during a break.

On a March night just before Easter, the Eliassons hosted two groups of Swedish performers who were visiting the city. Speaking before the performance, which was attended by some parents of the traveling students and friends of the embassy, Eliasson teased the parents that there was a "glow around you."

Then about thirty fifteen-year-olds from Stockholm's Adolf Fredrik School performed a selection of folkloric favorites. After a short break, the Lux Ensemble, a group of Swedes in their twenties, sang nineteenth-century classical selections. During both performances, Eliasson stood in the front row of listeners gathered around the singers, smiling broadly, swaying to music, looking on intently, and shouting "Bravo" when each number ended. He then spoke expansively about cultural diplomacy.

"I think you are our ambassadors," he told the performers. "I have the modest title of ambassador, but it hasn't always been translated into people-to-people communication. Music is a unifying force. You are united around the fact that we are all the same, we are equals. We have certain universal passions, and feel the liberation that comes from art and the beauty of music. Music is a powerful tool for uniting people.

"This is the best of cultural diplomacy. When diplomacy doesn't have that people-to-people contact acting as a unifying force, we lose a lot of energy. I want to see a massive exchange of culture and that will do wonders for us all."

ஃ V ஃ

Eliasson is intrigued by the notion of coming full circle—of ending a period in his life by enjoying a moment that recalls an earlier experience. So it was that the final formal dinner that Jan and Kerstin Eliasson held at their residence was before the 2005 Opera Ball.

The Brazilian embassy was hosting the late-evening reception with dessert and dancing. Sweden was one of several dozen embassies hosting a pre-party dinner. Eliasson in a black tuxedo mingled easily with his twenty guests, remembering names and telling anecdotes about his career in diplomacy. After escorting guests outside to gaze at the back of the residence and its magnificent lawn and garden, the ambassador and his wife led everyone to their dinning room.

After the meal, a representative from the Opera Ball thanked the Eliassons for hosting the event. The ambassador listened intently and then responded.

"This is our last dinner in this place. We've had five wonderful years. We've loved every minute of our time together. Several nights ago we walked around the residence and became sentimental. I became sentimental, Kerstin became melancholy," he said.

He then reflected on his time in Washington, representing the European Union during the Swedish presidency, and experiencing "the enormous tragedy of 9/11 and the aftermath of that we are all living with."

He recalled hosting the 2001 Opera Ball, joking that Princess Christina had him and Kerstin dancing until 2:30 in the morning. He reflected on his coming challenge as president of the UN General Assembly.

"I'm going to the UN with some trepidation and with humility. But I'm very proud that Sweden was asked to take on the presidency."

He said that Washington had changed in two ways since he was here in the 1970s—there is a more vibrant business community and there is a more substantial cultural life. Then he offered "a toast to friendship, to the opera, and to the Opera Ball, that you will all have a fun evening. And if I may say so, for a better and stronger UN."

CHAPTER 20

Fixed on the Far Horizon

Eliasson speaks to the UN General Assembly after his election as president.

🪾 **I** 🪾

On a spectacular April afternoon in Washington, the courtyard of the Johns Hopkins University School of Advanced International Studies is slowly coming to life. The dean of SAIS, Jessica Einhorn, and the president of Johns Hopkins, William Brody, are mingling with assorted dignitaries as they prepare to preside over a ceremony to dedicate a sculpture.

A few minutes before 4 p.m., Jan Eliasson strides into the sun-splashed courtyard in his trademark pinstripes, gold tie, and gold pocket hankie.

He moves through the crowd, shaking hands, and chatting easily with casually dressed students and the trustees of Johns Hopkins and members of SAIS's advisory board, who are in business attire.

This afternoon's ceremony combines two events that are important to Eliasson: the dedication of a replica of the *Single Form* sculpture and the Dag Hammarskjöld Memorial Lecture.

The sculpture is a half-size replica of the soaring, bronze abstract piece that stands on a granite plinth mounted on the site of the ornamental pool outside the United Nation's Secretariat building in New York. The original statue was the work of Barbara Hepworth and was unveiled in 1964 as a commemoration to Hammarskjöld, who served as head of the United Nations from April 1953 to September 1961 when he was killed in a plane crash while on a peace mission in the Congo. Hammarskjöld is revered in Sweden and the government organized a wide-ranging schedule of events in 2005 to celebrate the centenary of his birth.

Eliasson suggested to Einhorn that the dedication of the sculpture precede another significant event: a lecture by Brent Scowcroft, a respected member of the American foreign policy establishment, and a member of a blue-ribbon panel that just delivered an important report on UN reform. So on this day Swedish statesmanship and UN reform were joined in Washington.

Eliasson sits on the dais with the dignitaries, surveying the crowd for familiar faces. Einhorn introduces the ambassador as "a man of great humanitarian instincts" who will soon become president of the United Nation's General Assembly.

Eliasson uses his brief remarks to touch on themes that reflect his vision of the United Nations. He quotes Hepworth's words from the original dedication ceremony at the United Nations in 1964, arguing they are relevant and apt four decades later: "The United Nations is our conscience. If it succeeds it is our success. If it fails it is our failure."

He then lavishes praise on Hammarskjöld, calling him a role model not only for Swedish diplomats but for others in public service. Eliasson talks about Hammarskjöld's integrity, visionary support for preventive diplomacy, and creative role in establishing the United Nation's peacekeeping missions, which Eliasson believes are "one of the best functioning parts of the UN."

Drawing inspiration from Hammarskjöld's legacy and also looking ahead, Eliasson notes he will soon assume the daunting task of holding the presidency of the United Nation's General Assembly. Linking UN reform to other global challenges, Eliasson says that the world is at a crossroads in

Eliasson as UN undersecretary-general for humanitarian affairs in the early 1990s

which leaders must choose between multilateralism and unilateralism and also between hope and fear.

"Will we go to the future with more fear or more hope?" he asks, not sure of the answer. And then concluding his remarks, Eliasson quotes one of his favorite injunctions from Hammarskjöld—one that speaks to the ambassador's idealistic and yearning side: "Never look down to test the ground before taking your next step. Only he who keeps his eye fixed on the far horizon will find his right road."

After the ceremony, Eliasson talks with the special guests and lingers to chat with several students gathered around him, before he goes inside to the auditorium and sits in the front row to listen to Scowcroft make the case for significant but achievable UN reform.

❧ II ❧

For most of his career, Eliasson has been deeply interested in the United Nations—as many Swedish diplomats are. He served as Sweden's ambassador to the United Nations from 1988 to 1992 and was the first UN undersecretary general for humanitarian affairs. That job, he says, persuaded him about the urgent need for preventive diplomacy so that crises and massive suffering can be prevented.

As Sweden's deputy foreign minister and in other senior positions in Sweden's Foreign Ministry, he worked extensively on UN issues. He helped orchestrate Sweden's successful bid to win a seat on the UN Security Council in 1997–98. A photograph of a smiling Eliasson sitting at Sweden's desk in the United Nations after the vote was announced is one of his favorite pictures. Eliasson also devoted much of the 1980s to a UN-sanctioned mission to end the Iran-Iraq war.

Eliasson's friendship with UN Secretary General Kofi Annan goes back more than twenty years and includes a ritual New Year's Eve phone call to catch up on personal projects and discuss global affairs.

During much of Eliasson's time in Washington, UN issues were on the back burner for him as he focused on Sweden's bilateral relationship with the United States. The United Nations, however interesting and important, was not a central part of his Washington brief. But it was never far from his thoughts.

As he outlined Sweden's view of the world in dozens of private conversations and public events, he often cited the United Nations as a critical, if flawed, institution that could help craft multilateral solutions to pressing global problems.

Eliasson's most concrete involvement on UN issues during his early years in Washington came during the long and rancorous period before the American-led invasion of Iraq in 2003. Speaking for his government, Eliasson argued that absent an imminent attack from Iraq, only approval by the UN Security Council could make a U.S. invasion of Iraq legitimate. Eliasson repeated this argument forcefully and clearly in Washington and told administration officials that Sweden could not support a war against Iraq that did not have UN approval. He regularly articulated Sweden's views on the importance of UN support for an invasion and was noticeably displeased with the level and intensity of UN bashing that often occurred in the United States.

When President Bush's 2004 State of the Union speech took a swipe at the United Nations, Eliasson, from his chair in the diplomatic section on the floor of the House of Representatives, tightly folded his arms and looked down in frustration as lawmakers applauded. Eliasson subscribes to a vision of the United Nations that is popular in Sweden and was most comprehensively articulated by Hammarskjöld and the ambassador's former mentor, Olof Palme. That view asserts that working through the United Nations is the best way for Sweden to influence the international system and play a positive role in creating and preserving peace. From the Swedish perspective, the main task of the United Nations is to maintain peace and stability and to provide a forum where countries can discuss problems and resolve conflicts.

In a celebrated 1960 speech to the General Assembly, Hammarskjöld said the United Nations does not exist primarily to serve the interests of large states. Rather, the United Nations is especially valuable for small nations that need it for protection and for a place to express their views about world affairs. Nearly a quarter century later, Palme gave a speech in 1984 that outlined the four objectives of Sweden's UN policy: to promote respect for international law, defend human rights, press for the peaceful resolution of conflicts, and to work toward disarmament, especially nuclear disarmament.

Sweden has worked closely with the United Nations for decades, by offering its diplomats as mediators and experts, participating in peacekeeping operations, giving grants to UN agencies and activities, and participating in UN reform efforts and panels.

৯৯ III ৯৯

Eliasson's Washington involvement on UN issues changed significantly in November of 2004. At that time, he was endorsed to become president of the UN General Assembly by a group of western European countries and other nations that were set to hold the rotating presidency of the General Assembly in the next session of the UN. The United States strongly supported his nomination. The position went to a Swedish diplomat in large part to commemorate the one hundredth anniversary in 2005 of the birth of Hammarskjöld.

Sweden selected Eliasson as its nominee for the job. He is viewed as one of the country's best diplomats with considerable interest in, and knowledge of, UN issues. Additionally, he was strongly inclined to leave his job in Washington in the summer of 2005 making him available for the UN post.

"The offer and opportunity came out of the blue. At first I was really hesitant. It wasn't quite what I planned. But my wife helped persuade me I had to do it or I would spend the rest of my life regretting the decision. I've been telling her for the last twenty years that the UN needs to be reformed," Eliasson said.

Eliasson was formally elected president of the General Assembly on June 13, 2005, and assumed the presidency of the General Assembly on September 13, just as a much anticipated global summit convened under UN auspices in New York was about to begin. Eliasson's term as the president of the General Assembly runs for its sixtieth session, from September 2005 to September 2006.

With the General Assembly presidency awaiting him, Eliasson spent considerable time during his last six months in Washington working on UN issues. He kept two separate to-do lists—one for regular embassy activities and one for his UN work. Staffers at the embassy say that as his General Assembly presidency neared, his list of UN projects grew longer and his embassy list shorter.

Eliasson's nomination for the presidency of the General Assembly came at a time of considerable criticism of the United Nations and intense activity to craft plans for its overhaul. In September of 2003, Secretary General Kofi Annan told the General Assembly that the United Nations had reached a decisive time in its history and badly needed to be overhauled. He created a sixteen-person group to conduct a review, led by Thailand's former Prime Minister Anand Panyarachun, and including Scowcroft, to generate ideas about the policies and institutions required for the United Nations to work effectively in the twenty-first century.

The so-called High Level Panel on Threats, Challenges, and Change issued a report near the end of 2004 called "A More Secure World." It identified six clusters of threats that required new strategies and a reformed United Nations to confront: war between states; violence within states; poverty, infectious disease, and environmental degradation; the proliferation of weapons of mass destruction; terrorism; and transnational crime. It offered 101 recommendations to prevent wars, support development, combat poverty, fight terrorism, and bolster the United Nation's administrative machinery.

The panel said that a United Nations for the twenty-first century should have an expanded Security Council, a new peace building commission, better collaboration with regional groups, and give more powers to the Secretary General to manage the Secretariat and a new human rights panel.

Several months later, Annan, reeling from a mounting oil-for-food scandal, offered his own reform package based on the work of the High Level Panel. The Secretary General said that 2005 needed to be a year of bold decision and he offered a program that he called "In Larger Freedom." It urged global leaders to agree in the fall of 2005 on a plan to strengthen collective security, lay down a truly global strategy for development, advance human rights and democracy, and establish mechanisms to ensure that these commitments are translated into action. The United Nations, Annan said, must undergo the most sweeping overhaul of its sixty-year history. He challenged world leaders to recapture the spirit of San Francisco and forge a new world compact to advance the cause of larger freedom. A renewed United Nations, he said, needed major reforms to improve its relevance, effectiveness, and accountability. The General Assembly and Economic and Social Council needed to be strategic and purposeful in their work. And the Security Council should be expanded to include states that contribute most to the organization financially, militarily, and diplomatically.

Annan noted that there were two models to expand the Security Council from sixteen to twenty-four seats. One option was to create six new permanent seats and three new nonpermanent seats. An alternative approach would be to create nine new nonpermanent seats. Under either scenario, only the permanent seats of the United States, Russia, France, Great Britain, and China would retain their veto power in the Security Council.

❧ IV ❧

As these reform efforts were being developed and debated at the end of 2004 and the beginning of 2005, Eliasson assumed several different roles. As Sweden's ambassador to the United States he made it clear to American officials that his government supported the reform package offered by Annan. As the incoming president of the UN General Assembly, Eliasson kept in close touch with Scowcroft who had emerged as a respected American leader on UN issues, although one with increasingly strained relations with the Bush administration. Scowcroft still had good contacts with Republicans on Capitol Hill and was seen as a serious, credible, and practical advocate of UN reform.

The ambassador also intensified his discussions with senior Bush administration officials about overhauling the United Nations. He met with Nicholas Burns, the undersecretary of state for political affairs and with Philip Zelikow, the State Department's counselor about American views regarding UN reform.

He also traveled to Capitol Hill to gauge sentiment there. He met with Congressman Tom Lantos, the top Democrat on the House International Relations Committee, as well as staffers representing Senate Foreign Relations Committee Chairman Richard Lugar and Senator Chuck Hagel. Eliasson's overriding message was that the United Nations, though flawed in many ways, has accomplished many good things over six decades and would become more effective only if the United States participated constructively in its reform.

Eliasson also continued his work with Washington's think tank community, focusing much of his time and energy on projects related to UN reform.

He participated in seminars and conferences at the Brookings Institution, the Center for Strategic and International Studies, and especially the U.S. Institute of Peace, which had been mandated by Congress to conduct a study regarding American interests and UN reform. The task force was headed by former House Speaker Newt Gingrich and former Senate Majority Leader George Mitchell.

Eliasson attended UN-related seminars hosted by the Peace Institute and testified before the Gingrich-Mitchell panel. Eliasson believed the Gingrich-Mitchell report had the potential to fashion a bipartisan consensus in the United States on UN reform. Eliasson believed that there was little likelihood of UN reform without American support.

The Gingrich-Mitchell panel said it was struck by the United Nation's own receptivity to needed reforms, but added that a reform package had to be concrete, practical, and undertaken promptly. The panel urged far-reaching UN management reforms and refocused efforts to deal with key problems. But it advocated attention on actionable recommendations and urged the United Nations not to get tied down with an overly ambitious package that failed to win the necessary support.

The panel urged the Bush administration and Congress to embrace a comprehensive UN overhaul plan that included sweeping institutional reforms, more effective programs to fight terrorism and prevent proliferation of weapons of mass destruction, a strategy to improve the United Nation's capacity to stop genocide, support to bolster development, and improved capacity to conduct peacekeeping operations.

If Eliasson was engaged with the Gingrich-Mitchell panel, he carefully stayed out of the Senate's bruising confirmation battle over John Bolton's nomination for UN ambassador. When asked about the situation, Eliasson said he looked forward to working with whomever the United States sent to the United Nations.

ॐ **V** ॐ

In early June 2004, about a week before he was elected president of the UN General Assembly, Jan Eliasson traveled to a hotel in downtown Washington and devoted his Saturday morning to discussing UN reform before a friendly audience, the United Nations Association of the United States of America. The United Nations remained a favorite target for many American politicians and the House of Representatives was then poised to pass legislation that could result in withholding half of America's contributions.

In a speech taped by C-SPAN and broadcast on national TV several times, Eliasson said it was time to consider and pass a broad reform agenda in the United Nations. Interrupted by three standing ovations, Eliasson was preaching to the choir. But he also tried to inject realism into the discussion.

"These are difficult times for the UN. We have an uphill battle to present the UN in the light it deserves. I'm a friend of the UN, but not an uncritical friend," he said. "We have a problem in public opinion, but also in reality."

Eliasson lamented the considerable attention placed on the United Nation's failures, and the little appreciation for its important accomplishments in Afghanistan, Lebanon, Liberia, combating AIDS, helping refugees, and working for clean water.

"We must put the problem at the center," he said. The UN had a unique opportunity to enact significant and much needed reforms, he said.

"Do we have the political will to strengthen the UN and multilateralism?" he asked. "I'm still not sure we have enough political will to take the courageous and important steps ahead."

He acknowledged that Security Council reform was an important but also polarizing issue that could derail the entire reform project. Eliasson said he wanted the General Assembly to act more like a parliament with thematic debates and votes on meaningful not repetitive resolutions.

Enjoying his supportive and appreciative audience, Eliasson answered questions until he finally needed to hurry off and meet his wife at Dulles Airport.

✂ VI ✂

After a hectic, bittersweet weekend of farewell parties and receptions, Eliasson and his wife traveled to New York on Sunday, June 12. They went to the home of Kofi and Nane Annan for a visit and a glass of champagne in their garden. The next morning, June 13, Eliasson was unanimously elected president of the UN General Assembly for the term beginning on September 1, 2005. He was to be the presiding president during the United Nation's sixtieth anniversary year.

In a speech from the General Assembly's famous black marble podium, Eliasson praised Annan's reform effort as "the most comprehensive and cohesive proposal to strengthen the United Nations since the birth of the organization." He noted that the outgoing president of the General Assembly had transformed this proposal into a draft declaration to be considered in a few months. And then Eliasson returned to themes that emerged over a lifetime and were honed during his final six months in Washington.

"Today we are all facing a test of multilateralism. Will we develop the concepts and methods to deal with global problems in this age of rapid globalization?" he asked.

"Our main task is to accept and live up to the triple challenges of development, security and human rights. The three are intertwined and affect and reinforce each other."

He praised the "wisdom and far-sightedness" of the framers of the UN Charter. The ambassador said the measure for evaluating UN reforms must be the differences they make for people and crisis areas around the world: the starving child, the AIDS-stricken mother, the war-torn country, the polluted river, the desperate refugee, the unselfish humanitarian worker, the brave peacekeeping forces.

He said he would view all reforms in light of how they actually affect people on the ground. Eliasson said his experience as the UN undersecretary general for humanitarian affairs during the nightmare of Somalia in 1992–93 forever reminded him of the urgent need for prevention, for early action, and for effectively dealing with civil wars and the brutal ethnic and religious conflicts.

"We cannot, after Cambodia, Rwanda, Srebrenica, and Darfur, continue to say "never again" without seriously undermining the moral authority of the UN and its Charter." Eliasson said his General Assembly presidency would be guided by the values and principles that are pillars of Sweden's foreign policy: belief in multilateral cooperation; the imperative of prevention; respect for the rule of law and human rights; solidarity with the poor and persecuted; concern for the rights of women, for the children of the world and their future; and for the health of the environment.

"These aspirations, I know, are shared by people and nations in all regions of the world." Eliasson said there was an urgent need to offer international solutions and methods that correspond to the needs of today's world: fighting poverty, diseases, organized crime, trafficking, terrorism, proliferation of weapons of mass destruction, and environmental degradation, as well as preventing and resolving conflicts and stopping mass killing, torture, and abuse.

"This is the essence of the reform project of the UN: building a UN which effectively and legitimately responds to the urgent needs around the world and adds value to our work for security, prosperity and a life in dignity for all," he said.

And he closed his speech with his favorite Hammarskjöld injunction to look boldly into the future. "Never look down to test the ground before taking our next step: only he who keeps his eye fixed on the far horizon will find his right road."

CHAPTER 21

The Legacy

Jan and Kerstin at their summer home in Gotland

ৡ I ৡ

In our last formal interview, Jan Eliasson and I sat in his library at the ambassador's residence, which was once packed with books, strewn with papers, and full of photos of important moments in his personal life and professional career. Today the room, almost always bustling with energy, is quiet and mostly empty. There is nothing like the arrival of a moving van and a house full of boxes to concentrate the mind and encourage a person to reflect on the swift passage of time. The ambassador is subdued, soft-spoken, and tired from weeks of farewell lunches, dinners, meetings, and paperwork to close down his five years as Sweden's ambassador to Washington.

Eliasson recalls sitting in this same library more than thirty years earlier when a previous ambassador was preparing to leave Washington. Eliasson was the first secretary at the embassy and lived down the road. He was summoned to the residence on a weekend to help the ambassador compose his final report to Stockholm. Smiling at the memory, Eliasson remembers spending hours with the ambassador as he reminisced, served Manhattans ("that terrible drink"), and reflected on the state of the Swedish American relationship. Eliasson ended up drafting most of the report.

Eliasson acknowledges deep ambivalence about his departure from Washington—a city he knows well and loves. He has hundreds of personal friends, business contacts, and casual acquaintances in Washington. His daughter Anna, her husband Hector, and the ambassador's grandson Max, all live in DC.

"It's been a fascinating time. It's been a lot of fun. I feel better than when I arrived. I loved to be in charge. It's been my show. I feel greater vitality— professionally and personally—than I have before in a long time," he says.

"When you leave a place, a part of you dies. For me, it's one chapter closing and another beginning. It is a rich and fascinating chapter that is closing and an uncertain one is coming—with a completely different type of diplomacy," he says, referring to the UN post.

As he recalls his final full week in Washington, he vividly describes a farewell lunch at the Supreme Court prepared by Justice Sandra Day O'Connor and Dr. Martin Ginsburg, the husband of Justice Ruth Bader Ginsburg. Before the lunch, O'Connor took Jan and Kerstin Eliasson into the office of ailing Chief Justice William Rehnquist, who mused with Eliasson on his Swedish ancestry and expressed his appreciation for the eightieth birthday party the ambassador had hosted earlier that year at his residence. Eliasson said they felt sad as they left that meeting with Rehnquist, sensing they would not see the chief justice again. Rehnquist died a few months later.

৯৯ II ৯৯

For Eliasson, this is the end of a long transition that began more than six months earlier when he was nominated for the presidency of the General Assembly and began to wrap up his work in Washington and prepare for a new job in New York. While the ambassador worked harder than ever during his last half year in Washington, his staff sensed he was becoming less focused on Washington and more on the United Nations in New York. He became, despite inclination and temperament to the contrary, a lame duck.

Eliasson's successor, Gunnar Lund, visited Washington in the spring to meet with Eliasson, embassy staff, and others. Since his appointment as ambassador had not been officially approved by the American government, which is a ritual of bilateral diplomacy, Lund's trip was private and discreet. Most of the logistics were arranged by Caroline Vicini, the deputy chief of mission.

Eliasson brought Lund along to a private dinner he attended and introduced him to some contacts. Lund stayed at the residence and sized up his new home. The outgoing and incoming ambassadors played tennis and sat in the backyard, smoking cigars late into the night and talking about the job of ambassador to Washington.

Eliasson says he stressed how different diplomacy is in Washington than in other capitals. He emphasized the need to build a high-level network, in part through relentless social diplomacy, and then to cultivate that network carefully so it can be used to monitor the bilateral relationship and anticipate and solve problems.

Lund had been a government minister and headed up the Swedish delegations to the European Union. An experienced diplomat, he is an expert about the European Union but does not have extensive experience with the United States and its very specific diplomatic culture.

Some countries have elaborate mechanisms the outgoing ambassador employs to brief the incoming ambassador. For example, in a number of diplomatic corps, ambassadors are expected to compose a handing-over note that could reach a hundred pages in which the departing envoy outlines everything that he believes might be important for his successor.

Iran's system gives departing ambassadors several months and a quiet office to reflect on what they've learned at the post they have just left. They are expected to write a long essay that focuses on the large themes of their ambassadorship and their final impressions of the host country.

The Swedes have a surprisingly informal transition system. Eliasson met with Lund in Washington and discussed ongoing projects, major issues, and key personalities. But much of the actual transfer of information involved Eliasson debriefing Vicini who in turn briefed Lund. Eliasson drafted a report to Stockholm about U.S. foreign policy, but was swamped with the press of other business and didn't have a chance to compose a comprehensive review of the U.S.-Swedish relationship.

The final weeks of Eliasson's ambassadorship were full and bittersweet. There were elegant and impressive farewell parties such as the one hosted by the Kuwait ambassador Salem Abdullah Al-Sabah and his wife, Rima al-Sabah, which included many of Washington's political and cultural heavyweights. And there was a smaller, private party hosted by some personal friends that included Justices O'Connor and Ginsburg. There were playful songs, touching toasts, and music. Jan and Kerstin Eliasson danced to "New York, New York."

Eliasson's staff at the embassy held a surprise farewell party for him and gave him gag gifts including a photo spoof of the ambassador as James Bond. At the ambassador's final staff meeting, Vicini noted that this would be his final meeting as a full-time Swedish diplomat and offered warm words of praise for Eliasson and his work in Washington and elsewhere.

On his final day, after cleaning out his desk and saying good-bye to his comfortable office, the ambassador was walked to his car waiting outside the embassy by Monica Lundkvist, Gunilla Stone, and Claes Thorson. Several photographs that capture the departing Eliasson suggest weariness and a touch of sadness, as the ambassador concludes an important phase in his life and prepares for a new and uncertain one.

❦ III ❦

When asked to assess his ambassadorship, Eliasson says he recalls mostly a steady succession of projects, challenges, and interactions. "I think of it as a flow, not milestones," he says.

But when pressed he identifies important moments and events—helping prepare for three meetings between the Swedish prime minister and the American president, annual visits by members of Sweden's royal family, regular visits to Washington by Sweden's foreign and defense ministers and other senior government leaders, representing the European Union during the Swedish presidency, the tragic death of Anna Lindh, Nobel Prize receptions at the White House, and the terrorist attacks of September 11, 2001.

The ambassador says his wife was essential to his accomplishments in Washington. "Kerstin was absolutely crucial for establishing ourselves at the beginning. We have a little different styles—she takes a more low key role than I do—but she has an enormously winning personality. She built up important contacts from her two specialties—science and music—that were absolutely crucial for me. It was largely through her that I got to know Secretary Rice and Justice O'Connor on a personal level," he says.

So what was Eliasson's legacy?

Like virtually all ambassadors, Eliasson didn't leave his post as the architect of a landmark negotiation or the author of a sweeping foreign policy doctrine. That is not the job of the modern ambassador. Eliasson worked in a serious, professional way, day by day, to make sure that Stockholm understood what was going on in the most important country in the world and that the views of his nation were injected into the American policy debate. He often did this by presenting Sweden's perspective as reflective of the views of the European Union.

Throughout his years in Washington, Eliasson remained keenly interested in American life and followed developments in music, film, sports, and business. He was plugged in. But he focused his main energy on his central job: to develop high-level contacts within the American government and foreign policy apparatus. This allowed him to anticipate, prevent, and defuse tensions in Sweden's relationship with the United States. These contacts allowed him to alert Stockholm to what the world's only superpower was

The ambassador leaves his embassy for the last time.

about to do or say. These contacts also allowed him to explain Sweden's view of the world in the political capital of the world.

Through diligence, shrewdness, and charm, Eliasson made sure that Sweden was heard in Washington—even if it wasn't listened to. He assembled a network of contacts that made the Swedish embassy one of the most popular places on Embassy Row.

Eliasson left behind a feeling of goodwill toward his country, and solid connections with the administration, State Department, Congress, the think tank world, and the Swedish American community.

"Jan is not a theoretician," one of his staffers at the embassy said in summarizing his accomplishments. "He doesn't write a lot of complex articles and books about the theory of international relations. But he has a very smart, very shrewd, very practical approach to solving problems—or preventing issues from becoming problems. He is a very good professional. He has a great instinct for how decisions are made both in Washington and Stockholm, who made them, and at what time and in what way he could influence them. It's a very great skill. He's very, very good at what he does. There are not many who are better."

SOURCES

This book is largely based on two years of interviews and reporting. In addition to my interviews with Ambassador Eliasson, I conducted nearly 100 interviews with Swedish and American diplomats, government officials, and experts in diplomacy.

I did extensive research on the role of the modern ambassador, reading all that was available. The works I consulted are listed below. I would like to highlight the writings of Kishan Rana, a former Indian diplomat, who has written extensively and insightfully on the changing role of the ambassador. I had two extensive and enjoyable interviews with Ambassador Rana in the summer of 2005 when he was in Washington as a fellow at the Woodrow Wilson Center.

This book also required that I immerse myself in Swedish foreign policy and diplomacy. The American Swedish Institute offers a great deal of helpful information on its website: www.americanswedishinst.org.

The Swedish embassy's website provides important background information on Sweden and access to official government documents: www.swedenabroad.com/washington.

Other helpful websites are: the Swedish Trade Council (www.swedishtrade.com/usa/), Invest in Sweden Agency (www.isa.se/), Swedish Council of America (www.swedishcouncil.org), and the Swedish-American Chamber of Commerce (www.sacc-usa.org).

The books I found most helpful are:

Berridge, G.R. *Diplomacy: Theory and Practice.* Palgrave Macmillan, Basingstoke, UK, 2002.

Briggs, Ellis O. *Proud Servant: The Memoirs of a Career Ambassador.* The Kent State University Press, OH, 1998.

Catto, Henry. *Ambassadors at Sea: The High And Low Adventures of a Diplomat.* University of Texas Press, TX, 1998.

Craig, Gordon A. and Gilbert, Felix, editors. *The Diplomats, 1919–1939.* Princeton University Press, NJ, 1953.

De Callieres, Francois. *On the Manner of Negotiating With Princes.* Houghton Mifflin Company, MA, 2000. First published in 1716 in France.

Eban, Abba. *Diplomacy for the Next Century.* Yale University Press, CT, 1998.

Freeman, Chas W., Jr. *The Diplomat's Dictionary.* United States Institute of Peace Press, Washington, DC, 1997.

Gotlieb, Allan. *I'll Be With You in a Minute Mr. Ambassador: The Education of a Canadian Diplomat in Washington.* University of Toronto Press, Canada, 1991.

Herz, Martin F. *215 Days in the Life of an American Ambassador.* Institute for the Study of Diplomacy, Washington, DC, 1981.

Herz, Martin F., editor. *The Modern Ambassador.* Institute for the Study of Diplomacy, Washington, DC, 1982.

Lankford, Nelson D. *The Last American Aristocrat: The Biography of David K.E. Bruce.* Little, Brown and Company, MA, 1996.

Mayer, Martin. *The Diplomats.* Doubleday and Company, NY, 1983.

Meyer, Christopher. *DC Confidential: The Controversial Memoirs of Britain's Ambassador to the U.S. at the time of 9/11 and the Iraq War.* Weidenfeld & Nicholson, London, UK, 2005.

Miller, Hope Ridings. *Embassy Row: The Life and Times of Diplomatic Washington.* Holt, Rinehart and Winston, NY, 1969.

Nicholson, Harold. *Diplomacy.* Institute for the Study of Diplomacy, 1988. First published in the Home University Library, 1939.

Nickles, David Paul. *Under the Wire: How the Telegraph Changed Diplomacy.* Harvard University Press, MA, 2003.

Polk, William R. *Neighbors and Strangers: The Fundamentals of Foreign Affairs.* The University of Chicago Press, IL, 1997.

Rana, Kishan S. *The 21st Century Ambassador: Plenipotentiary to Chief Executive.* Diplo-Foundation, Malta, 2004.

Rana, Kishan S. *Bilateral Diplomacy.* DiploHandbooks, Malta, 2002.

Riordan, Shaun. *The New Diplomacy.* Polity Press, Cambridge, UK, 2003.

Scott, Gail. *Diplomatic Dance: The New Embassy Life in America.* Fulcrum Publishing, CO, 1999.

Smith, James Allen. *The Idea Brokers: Think Tanks and the Rise of the New Policy Elite.* Free Press, NY, 1991.